I dedicate this book to my God
and my Wendy

To Him be the Glory!

Groanings...

Romans 8:26 speaks of the Holy Spirit and how He intercedes for us with groanings too deep for words when we simply do not know how to pray. I feel that way about trying to find words to describe how thankful I am to the people I will now mention. While there are certainly hundreds of people literally around the world who influenced and inspired me as I wrote and pondered and prayed through this book, there were a few who prayed for me and ministered to me and invested in my life in ways that I could never compensate. Greg Golden put aside his personal preferences, his pride, and his own views on life, to objectively wade through what was a very harsh and distasteful early draft of the book you have in your hands. His love for Christ and his love for people is unlike anything I've ever experienced in my walk with God. He is the epitome of loving people and I love and appreciate him for being my friend and my brother in Christ. In the past few years, nearly every sermon that I heard Pastor Alan Floyd preach spoke to me with regard to the contents of this book. His dedication to the truth of God's Word and His love for God and His people were a constant reminder to me of just why I was writing, of just why I was seeking to be obedient no matter the cost. In my prayers for Alan Floyd, I saw God move in powerful ways through his messages and especially through his personal interactions with me. Bo Gunn really came into my life through conversations about and a love we shared for C. S. Lewis and his book Mere Christianity. Through many early Saturday mornings at the local Waffle House and texts and calls, this man became a prayer warrior for me in the struggle to stay the course with this book - to be obedient to God's clear direction. As Bo led our life group on Sunday mornings, our conversations and his insight into God's Word were a constant source of inspiration and truth. I could never have survived the doubt and frustration of such an undertaking without this dear brother in my life. Thank you Bo! The second woman to dive into the depths of these pages was none other than my own dear mother, who herself is a survivor of breast cancer. I will never know how many hours my Mama spent in prayer for me over the last few years, but I know she was truly a biased reviewer. Mama and I have developed a relationship with each other and with God at the center that has brought us closer and dearer to one another than I ever thought possible. She loves me and my brother unconditionally, and this I know is true regardless of the content of this book. I love you Mama.

Wendy....

There were numerous opportunities for this woman to give up on me, to do away with me, to walk away, to have me committed, even to have me taken out! On many occasions she would have been well justified to do so. She did not. We're still together as husband and wife. She instead chose to rise to the occasion, to dig into God's Word, to pray, to seek, to change, to hold on, to go against the grain, in some cases to go against her wise counsel ....and to love. We are still very different people, but we are still one. I am forever indebted to this creature because without her, I don't know that I would have ever really worked out my own faith. I remember also, that on at least one occasion, I believe she literally saved my life. I love you my beautiful, wonderful, fascinating, wife. All things are possible with God. Thank you.

Genuine

We Don't Know What We Don't Know

I am an engineer by degree and conception so to speak. To say that I am analytical is to say the sun is a twinkle. I question everything. You could spend your time trying to convince me that something is or isn't fully functional, but I'm *still* going to investigate it for myself. I look for and question even the already existing solutions to every problem I see. I question the methods, the research, and I wonder about the reasons and complexities that may have been overlooked. Are what we think we *know* to be the best approaches and the methods simply the only ones that have been examined? Are there better solutions to expired problems that seem to fail, but are simply misunderstood or overlooked? Are the standards we maintain for beauty, healthcare, and living really the *most effective* ones obtainable, or simply the ones that we have settled for in our confused culture? Are the limitations that we place on our lives really the ones defined by God and his Word, or have we *unintentionally* allowed the world to enforce its boundaries and rules upon us? In 1 Corinthians 4:6 we see Paul warn the Corinthian Church - I have applied all these things to myself and Apollos for your benefit, brothers, that you may learn by us not to go beyond what is written, that none of you may be puffed up in favor of one against another. Clearly, this problem must have even existed even back in Paul's day, with some of those early church leaders bowing to the ways of the world instead of God's Word. This book materialized when I applied my analytical thinking to the problems I experienced in my own life and what I believe to be God's will and calling on my journey with Him. You can trust that I don't have the mental capacity to dazzle you with my exquisite use of the English language, nor am I going to present to you any new or mind-blowing ideas, necessarily. I am *just* a man and an engineer for goodness sake! In fact, much of the content actually comes from other like-minded people, and I have been careful to give each of them their due credit for thoughts that were not my own. I was really not sure of the inclination to write a book when I first got started. However, as I have been researching, studying, praying, and writing over these many months and years, I continue to pray and ask God to reveal to me His purpose in it.... and I believe that He has. I've also seen His hand at work in my life and the lives of those who have reviewed the manuscript for me. Throughout the book, I will remind you that I certainly do not claim to have all the answers, but maybe I can provide you with enough information as to motivate you into action and study for yourself in some given area – maybe even one that I've not touched on myself. This is really my hope, and honestly, I pray that it is God's will for you and for me. Not that I convince you to step to one side or the other of any given issue, but that I persuade you to at least seek to know how you formed your convictions and why you do what you do. So, do not *allow* me, through this book, to transform your convictions on one issue or another, but rather allow God and His perfect Word to set the standards for your life. If your convictions and your walk with the Lord are truly of His divine will for your life, then far be it from me to lead you away from that. However, in these deceptive times, we must have certainty that we have indeed heard from God, be sure that we know and understand exactly what His Word says, and be *sure* the path we choose is one that is GENUINE. Be cautious that you have not built your convictions upon a foundation based on popular culture, or tradition or convention - even those within the church. As the Word says in Matthew 7:13, the gate is wide and the path is easy that leads to destruction. Now prepare yourself, for some of you this will be a bit of a radical journey. I believe for many of you, it will simply be a breath of very fresh air!

And now for Bo....the preface

What if I told you that much of what has been instilled in you about life and living is completely false? Could you face that reality? The more important question, would you dare to face that reality? What if in fact these deceptions have been propagated with good intention by the very people who are closest to you and seemingly love you the most? What if some trivial, seemingly meaningless detail in your life that was intended to enhance it, is actually destroying it? What if some of the very ways that you have been programmed to live in order to have a good and Godly life, are the very things that have led you and others astray? What if the very cultural norms and conventions that we have purposefully maintained are the very things that have facilitated the demise of our world into immorality, turmoil, and disease? What if some of the conventions instilled in us over the last hundred years in an effort to sustain life or reduce the physical demands on our bodies are actually the cause for some of our health epidemics? What if the very means by which we strive to conserve time in our lives are the very same things that are stealing it? If there is truth to be found in some of the answers to these questions, would you be courageous enough, strong enough, deliberate enough, and Godly enough to take a stand and move in a direction *opposed* to the world, society, culture, tradition, your church, your government, your friends, your family or even your spouse? Could you stand up to the criticism, embarrassment, and shame that would be thrust upon you like a giant wave breaking onto a beach? What if like Abraham, when he set out to sacrifice his son Isaac, God asked you to step out into the darkness and do something or change something or challenge something that is beyond reason, common sense, or comprehension? What would you do?

The tendency as you read this book, especially for the women, might be to feel condemned about the conventions you practice or the way you live - *that could not be farther from the intent of my heart*! You are likely to be offended very easily given the topics I cover. But the Bible says in 1 Corinthians 3:19 – "For the wisdom of this world is folly with God". In Luke 16:15 Jesus says "what is exalted among men is an abomination in the sight of God". Open your eyes to the possibility that you have been programmed, deceived by the world, into thinking that your current way of life is an absolute, and that you chose it, instead of *it choosing you*. Open-your-eyes-to-the-possibility-that-you-have-been-programmed,-deceived-by-the-world,-into-thinking-that-your-current-way-of-life-is-an-absolute,-and-that-you-chose-it,-instead-of-*it-choosing-you*. So much counterfeit information about how we live, our hygiene, our clothes, our attitudes about our bodies and sexuality has been propagated down through the years that we've come to accept it as truth, when in reality much of it is false and fabricated. It's not at all *genuine*. For the most part, this is no fault of yours or mine, but how you choose to live once you can see the *genuine* truth rests on *your* conscience. Not only that, but what you teach your children and how you allow the world to continue to program them will be your responsibility as well. I've read hundreds, if not thousands, of stories about people who have stepped away from convention and cultural norms and were very *pleasantly* surprised at the outcome. In fact, I have done this in my own life and have experienced many *improvements* in the quality of my daily life in a variety of ways. I urge you, as you read through each chapter of this book, come back to this preface and reload these opening paragraphs into your mind. Decide for yourself with God's Word and guidance - without any influence from the world or culture or family - how you will live your life. Let your thoughts and actions be driven only by God and His perfect Word and the ability He gave you to reason and think for YOURSELF. This will be no easy task – you will have to purpose to do this. I know that you will be glad IF you do.

I use quite a bit of *italics*, please give those words special attention as they are key in the points that I attempt to communicate.

VIII

Why even write a book regarding so many controversial Topics?

God says in His Word that He wants us to have life, but not just life, not just muddle through, not just barely survive - He says that His desire is for us to have an ABUNDANT life or have it to the *fullest* extent possible! – John 10:10. How many of us are really *doing* that? Pursuing that? In every area of our life? Are we *actively* playing a role in living out that abundant life? Or are we just going with the flow and going through the motions – muddling through? We aren't meant to just muddle through - the Word says that we should work out our faith – we have to "do". (James 2:17; Philippians 2:12-13) As we wait for the return of Jesus and generations of men and women live out their lives here on earth - fashion, culture, and tradition expand and change and often function to rob us of that abundant life, *and we don't even know it*. This book is an attempt to dispel and disprove some of these traditions and myths with regard to the world and God's Word and His desire for us to live out the abundant life. The longer I live, the more apt I am to challenge everything around me to be sure that what I perceive to be true... - is really *the* truth. Winston Churchill once said, "*Truth is incontrovertible. Panic may resent it, ignorance may deride it, malice may distort it, but there it is.*" So many of us live our lives today based on conventions or customs and practices that sooner or later take us down some erroneous paths, *and we don't even know it*. Many times, they deprive us of the abundant life - *and we don't even know it!* Here is a real-life example of how such assumptions not only keep us from all that God has for us, but sometimes they can even bring unnecessary stress and frustration into our lives.

Our oldest son was about to start his first year of college, and I had rented a trailer with plans to move him from home to an apartment 250 miles away one weekend. I had also just purchased an older, lifted, truck and I had been working out some of the "kinks" with it for about a month or so. One of the improvements that I had just made was to cover the wheel-wells with thick rubber guards as to deflect mud off the engine and underside of the truck. Prior to this modification, I had been driving the truck without any real problems for a couple of months or so. My family and I departed late one afternoon pulling the trailer, headed for the apartment and all seemed fine for about the first 15 miles or so. All of a sudden, we heard this awful vibration commence from what sounded like the front driver's side tire. I pulled off the interstate at the very next exit and my son and I jumped out of the truck to inspect the tire and wheel-well. There were several flaps of the rubber wheel-well guard that were somewhat loosely hanging down over the suspension, but were prime candidates for the cause of the horrific noise. We trimmed them back in hopes that they were the source of the annoyance. We got back on the interstate only to hear the clamor commence again at about 60mph or so. The noise was definitely a result of the wind blowing over something loose as it only started at speeds above 50mph and then would stop when we slowed to speeds less than that. A few miles further down the road we pull off again to do a little more trimming and see if we could make any other adjustments that might stop the noise. Back on the road, the noise was louder than ever and all five of us were certain that it was coming from the area near the driver's side front wheel – seemingly right under the floorboard behind the pedals. We decided to just drive until we had to stop again for fuel or a restroom and then we'd take another look. This time I opened the hood to see if maybe the source of the noise was something loose inside the engine compartment against the firewall. We tried some duct tape to see if we could stiffen up the tab of rubber material that seemed to be loosely flapping in the wind. We finally just endured the noise for the remainder of the trip with plans to take a closer look once we had a good night's sleep. The next afternoon I went through several iterations of engineering bungee cords and foam and duct tape in a variety of arrangements to see if I could quiet or alleviate the problem. My younger son and I took the truck on several test-runs after each such alteration only to find the noise still going strong, and even getting louder. Having given up on finding a temporary resolution to the annoyance, the next day my family and I just struggled through the loud, maddening ride home over the next several hours. It was exasperating to say the least.

Once home, I began making one little change at a time followed by a test drive to see if I could finally nail down the source. I used a bungee cord and some vice-grip pliers to secure a little flap here and there, one way then another, the front-the middle-the back – where is this coming from!??? On the way back to the house on one of several such test drives, with plans to just completely remove the rubber guards altogether, the noise had started back up as it had been doing now for three days. For some reason during this drive, I reached up and touched the windshield with my fingertips. As soon as I felt the vibration in the windshield, I knew immediately that the source of the noise was definitely NOT in the wheel-well at all. Because the sound was traveling through the windshield and coming from below the dash and because I had just completed the wheel-well covering job, we were all *"certain"* that this was the problem. Never once in the three days of driving had we even looked at the windshield or *inspected any other area of the truck*. I had performed an intense cleaning of the windshield just prior to us leaving for the road trip. In doing so I must have loosened a little of the weather-stripping near the top, and it had worked its way further and further out and was making more and more noise dancing in the wind as the truck moved faster and faster down the road. *At any point on during the three-day trip*, I could have simply reached up and tucked the weather-stripping back into the gap around the windshield and eliminated the noise completely – no tools, no duct tape, no bungee cords, no engineering, ...just my bare hands. (By the way, after simply tucking the weather-stripping back into the gap the truck has been quiet to this day – nearly a year later!) We had tried foam, bungee cords, vice-grips, duct tape and all sorts of ideas, but ultimately none of these ever helped the situation. Why? Mostly because we stuck with the original *assumption* that the newly installed wheel-well guards were the problem (what we thought was true), we had never broadened the scope of our search enough to find the *real* source of our grief. We suffered through 3 days of frustration and irritation when the resolution was quick and simple and literally right in front of my face the whole time I was driving. *How often is this scenario played out in just living life, though most of the time with much more significant issues and problems?* How often do our assumptions and traditions and cultural norms and practices with regard to the Bible, people, appearances and righteousness serve only to be unnecessary, and even unbiblical frustrations in our lives? How often do we just resolve to live with the status quo rather than stepping outside the constraints and choosing to go in a new direction, with a new solution, or a new way of doing something in pursuit of the abundant life? *How often?* Unfortunately, the answer is *ALL of the time.*

We come into this world and we're really taught from a very young age about all of these life "givens" that we just shouldn't question. While this may be beneficial for us as children, we carry so much of this mentality into our adult lives and then it often robs us of the abundant life. Here's another very practical example of how such thinking can be detrimental. One very foggy morning we departed home for church and I was driving my wife's car. It has this "auto" setting on the headlight control knob that I don't really care for because I like to be in control! And I just don't trust the car to make the right decisions for me with regard to the lights. As we departed, I asked my wife if the car was "aware" of the fog and thus would turn the lights on in the auto mode? She didn't really answer me, but I could tell that this aggravated her because she knew I didn't trust the auto. So being me, I pulled off the road just a short distance from our house and got out of the car to see if the lights were really "on". They were not. Aha! We should have assumed that they were, but they were not. As we passed dozens of cars coming at us through the fog that morning, many of them didn't have any lights on. I now wonder how many of those people are trusting the "auto"? What a huge risk they are taking with their lives as they drive down the road – and most probably don't even know it. How many of you are trusting the "auto" mode, the "givens", with the issues of life? What if it's letting you down, and you don't even know it? What if the stakes are very high with risk of trusting convention and culture and you don't even know it?

How often do we Christians do this very thing with the Word of God? Or even the church? We just trust that the programming we receive is good, Godly and beneficial. That we don't even need to question it. That it "must" be right. *Surely* what's been taught for hundreds of years in the church is biblical, is Godly, and is genuine. We never even think about or question so many of these things, and that is *exactly* what the enemy wants. He wants us in "coast" mode. Don't question anything. Don't seek Godly wisdom on any *"settled"* matter. Don't examine His Word in an effort to know the truth. Don't draw close to Him to understand. Just trust what you've been told and leave God and the Bible out of it. If Satan can just get us to go with the flow, he can keep us right where he wants us - missing out on God's blessing, on God's truly abundant life that he promises. Many times, we just keep going down a path that can and does lead to physical and even spiritual death for us and our loved ones. This is exactly what the Pharisees and Sadducees did with regard to Jesus, they trusted in their tradition, their culture, their way of life, without ever examining or seeking the truth.

This book is an attempt to deal with a few very *controversial* topics that have affected my life and maybe yours in some way. I'll go ahead and tell you (unless you looked ahead), many of the topics in this book have more of a focus on women than men, but the effects on relationships and marriages can be far reaching nonetheless. The writing here will be based on input from me, various Internet blogs, surveys, pastors, sermons, other books, the Bible and the interactions with people around me in my everyday life (though names will be omitted to protect the innocent). Through my wife, daughter and other females in my life, I have developed somewhat of a keen sense for peering a little deeper into the everyday issues of women. Not that men don't have any issues, but let's face it, women have far more scrutiny on them with regard to our western culture and society than do men. There is undoubtedly far more information to be discovered and uncovered with regard to each of the topics I'll mention, but the idea was to provide a glimpse into a few troublesome areas. The hope is that you, the reader, will follow up with your own research into any given interest and continue to learn even more beyond what you find here. Study God's Word. Live your life. Don't let tradition, popular culture, opinion or hearsay *determine* your existence. Do! Act! Move! In the book Mere Christianity, it was said of C. S. Lewis that he felt a *complacent acceptance of the status quo reflected more than a failure of nerve*. Many of you are so bound up with unnecessary worries and concerns about how you should look, or what you should (or should not) wear, if your hair is gray, does this outfit make me look fat, should I straighten my hair or curl it, and the list goes on and on and on. There's a popular song - "Already Gone" by the Eagles - with a line that says "so oftentimes it happens that we live our lives in chains, that we never even know we have the key". How true is that for so many of us in so many ways? How sad it would be to get to the end of your life and *then realize* that many of the restrictions and limitations you placed on yourself were irrelevant, or even detrimental in some way. God gave us the keys to unlock many of the chains in our lives that keep us bound up, if we'll just *choose* to use them. For that matter, we've allowed man to put so many chains on us that God never intended for us to carry. Sadly, we are now blind, deaf, and bound in a lot of ways and have just accepted this *without challenge* as being "necessary" to our "way of life". A friend of mine posted this statement online this morning – "we better know the truth because the truth always sets us free". The most important part of this statement is that we must first KNOW the truth – we must have eyes to see the truth. Tradition, culture, society, the Church and *even* mama can sometimes lead us astray by declaring an adulterated version of the "truth". Get into the Word, make sure that what you *"believe"* to be true – *is indeed the truth.*

Knowing the truth isn't really the end of the journey, *accepting* the truth can be just as much or more of a challenge for many. Let me give you an example. It has been scientifically *proven* that many of the artificial sweeteners used today are really worse for your health than the sugar that they replace. In fact, some research has shown that your body actually stores *more* fat when you drink the diet soda over long periods of time. There's a myriad of reasons why artificial sweeteners are bad for you – that's been well established. So health-wise, you're probably better off to drink the regular sugar-sweetened soda vs. the diet in the interest of weight-loss and health. Now whether you believe that or not, and really whether this is really true or not, is irrelevant for my example. Let's just assume for the sake of this example that we can *know* for certain that this is indeed the *truth*. Let's also assume that a person considers this and does some research and comes to understand for themselves that this is *indeed* the *truth*. If the individual began drinking diet soda in an effort to lose or maintain weight, and thus sustain their health, then wouldn't they carry this premise through to give up the diet soda in exchange for the regular *in light of the scientific truth?* Maybe not. Though they know that the diet drink is even worse for them health-wise than the sugared soda, they choose to continue to drink the diet because it is a well-established habit and they have acquired a taste for it. Not only that, but if they were to make a change, how would they explain it to the watching world around them? It could be embarrassing for them to admit that what they've believed and what they have been practicing for years and years was... incorrect, wrong, and actually harmful to them. This, I believe, was the main issue with the Pharisees and Sadducees of Jesus' day. Even if they had doubts about "their" truth, about their traditions, about their law, they could not bring themselves to admit to this – it would be far too embarrassing. They have not *accepted* the truth, though they still *know* the truth. I believe that this is exactly how God sees sin in our lives. We often know "the" truth, HIS truth, but yet we decide to go against it and against Him *anyway*. We do not accept His truth when we do this, although we certainly *know* it.

I realize that I am a bit unusual, unconventional, irregular, abnormal and just flat-out weird when it comes to my observations and notions about the world around me. (At least compared to the crowd and todays Western culture!) However, it is my hope that some of these thoughts provide an opportunity for growth and a renewed interest in making some changes in your life, changes that would take you down a path of a *more* abundant life!

Before we begin, I must warn you that my discussion of matters beyond this point is very frank, very blunt, very honest, but also very genuine. Many of you may find yourself in a bit of a rage after reading some of the things I have to say, but yet still may not be able to dispute the *truth* in what I've brought to your attention. While I'm not *absolutely* sure of some of the content in the pages of this book (with the exception of the scripture quoted), I am absolutely sure that God led me to share it with you for His good purpose. If at any point in reading this book you feel offended, I simply ask you to stop and do one thing – ask yourself why? ... And give an honest answer. As I have already mentioned, it is not my goal or purpose to offend you, but some of you will certainly be offended. You can choose to toss this book in the trash and muddle on, or you can choose to change your mind. You can choose to let the truth set you free, or you can choose to crucify it. Now open your mind, try to release your worldly inhibitions, and prepare for a journey into the anti-culture! You cannot say that I didn't warn you. Here we go!

1 Where and how did we get off track?

We should start with what many would consider the most challenging, really the most awkward, subject first. Read these words aloud to yourself: sex, vagina, vulva, labia, clitoris, penis, testicles, anus, buttocks, breasts, nipples, areola.... (Now did you *really* read them out loud? Don't cheat!) These words and the mention of the anatomical members of the human anatomy can summon fear, embarrassment, humiliation and shame in many, if not most, Christians, pastors, parents, and a wide variety of other folks – even when sitting alone in an empty room. (You may have just felt a little shame and embarrassment yourself, even though you probably didn't read these words out loud) Why? With very little exception (if any at all), everyone on the face of the planet has either the male or female composition of the human anatomy listed. Not to mention that our bodies and their parts and functions were *not* the invention of a sinful, lustful, and mortal man, but rather a loving and perfect Creator. After the creation, He then looked at our fleshly bodies and called them "good". God declared our bodies good. He *still* declares our bodies good. Truth be known, most of us cannot accept that. We may say we do, but our lifestyles and actions prove otherwise. For Christians, we believe that a sovereign, omnipotent, omniscient, omnipresent God brought us into being in a culmination of creation that concluded with the physique of the very first woman, Eve. So how do we go from the very pinnacle of God's creation – the most incredible, beautiful, magnificent, intricate creature on earth – to the point where we (mostly Christians and some other "religious" people) do everything we can to shame, cover, conceal, camouflage, disguise, augment, contort, mask, and *improve* upon His already declared *good* work? Good question, huh? You might say, with all of the blatant sensuality, pornography, lustfulness, and lewdness of the world, we just don't have much of a choice with how we "view" the human body – especially the female. What if we do? Or a better question might be, what if we had not already traveled so far down what could be a wrong road? What if instead of just hiding, shaming, and disguising the body we brought meaning, beauty, understanding, and acceptance of the body to the next generation? What if we communicated the *good* of God's good creation instead of just the bad with regard to how the world has perverted it? Given that the woman is the pinnacle of God's creation, wouldn't it make sense that Satan would rage a war against her in every way possible? What if by concealing, disguising, and "adorning" the human body we have really only served to teach *unnecessary* shame, inhibition and confusion? What would we convey to the world, as Christians, if we regarded the human body as incredible and beautiful and our sexuality as truly a gift from God instead of a shame? What if we stopped teaching our kids (especially our girls) that they should be ashamed of their bodies, that their natural, normal shape and form is somehow automatically lewd? What if we *stopped* teaching them that their appearance, as created by God, *isn't nearly good enough?* Could our actions as Christians, as "good" people, as "Godly" people be somewhat responsible for the unhealthy, unbiblical, and immoral sexual deviance and shame that is intensifying in our country and around the world? Pastor David Hatton states it better than I can – "Evangelical 'pulpiteers' can shout louder than ever about sexual morality, but most are still reluctant to frankly address the physical aspects of human sexuality, even at a time when society *desperately* needs to hear a Christian voice. Why this characteristic shyness about sex? Believers have no biblical warrant for it. Such a squeamish attitude certainly didn't come from our Maker. Neither in Scripture nor in orthodox Christian theology is there even a shred of support for our long history of embarrassment about the body's sexual nature. In fact, a careful review of the Bible itself—done in the fear of God and not in the fear of tradition—will actually show that our reasons for avoiding the anatomy of gender and its physiological purposes in sexuality are not only unscriptural, but may have heretical roots."[1] I don't know about you, but I had never thought about this as being one of our "desperate" needs before. But with a bit of careful, objective study, I think you will agree that it certainly is.

Some of you are already beginning to walk through this now in your mind, and you're asking the question, "So what are you saying Bosarge, should we just take off all our clothes and run naked?" (Wouldn't that be exhilarating! ...Well, maybe for some) Would this really help resolve the sexual disparity of our day? Well no, at this point in time, a leap to simple social nudity would certainly not be a positive attempt to resolve the

---

[1] David Hatton – 2012 -
http://pastordavidrn.blogspot.com/2012/07/seq-chapter-h-r-1-sexis-central-to-gods.html

sexual tension in our culture. However, we could reconsider the way in which we indoctrinate our children so that we raise a future generation of Christian young men and women who have a *healthy* and *Godly* appreciation, respect, and love for His most incredible masterpiece. Instead, we currently have a generation of young people (especially the girls) who are shamefully aware of their bodies and all of the "flaws" and curves and protrusions and oddities that must be hidden or masked or augmented, or shaved, or concealed - for what? Why? ...Well I'll get into that later on, but for now let's just step back in time a few hundred or thousand years and see what has changed and what has remained the same. Now for the sake of argument, it really doesn't matter how far back we travel, as the information found in this book will be based on the Word of God, logic and common sense – NOT culture or time or tradition.

Some of you are already shaking your head saying "boy, this guy is way off track". That could be, as I too am simply a mortal, sinful man just like you. Ultimately, I don't really care if you *agree* with me or not. My hope is to stimulate your mind regarding your views, beliefs, and convictions and their *origins* and *authenticity* with regard to God, the Bible and your fellow man. It could be that your feelings about sex, modesty, nudity and the human body are based mostly on tradition, cultural norms, convention, or misinterpretation, and *not at all* on the *truth* of God's Word. As my pastor recently stated - "You are wrong if you think you know everything you need to know". So much of what we have been taught as the "truth" is nothing more than tradition, culture, or simply ignorant knowledge that has been passed down from generation to generation. We unknowingly crafted it to be "truth" only because that's what we've been told by the people we trust the most, and we simply have never questioned it. So many of us wake up every day and go through the motions of life without ever stopping to ask why. Why do we do the things we do? Why do we avoid the things we avoid? How and why do we place value on what the world thinks of us in terms of our appearance or our faith? Paul gives a stern warning for us with regard to our faith and our reasoning in Galatians 1:9 – If anyone is preaching to you a gospel contrary to the one you received, let him be accursed. Certainly *not* to add to what Paul was saying, but I would go one step farther and say that if anyone is teaching you a morality or standards that are not in the Word, then *why* be bound by them? Jesus was certainly *not* bound by the traditions, customs, and practices of the Pharisees, in fact He challenged them all – and they killed him for it.

Ultimately, Christians simply strive to grow closer to God through serving our fellow man as we spread the Gospel and do this within the bounds of God's Word. I'm not in any way advocating that we stray from the Word or God's will or the core beliefs of our Christian faith, but I am asking you to begin to think about some of the stigmas, stereotypes, and practices that you have come to accept as the "Christian" way or the "truth". Are all of these based on the Word of God and our genuine faith? Or have we accepted some of them as genuine and true simply because they were handed down to us from the church, or pastors, or parents? Could some of your own personal convictions be based on lies and deceit? To turn from such long-held beliefs and go in a seemingly opposite direction, one that is completely opposed to what "has been" in generations past, can be a frightening proposition. What will my friends think? What will my parents think? What will my church friends think? Will they still accept me? Will they ridicule me? Will they challenge me? These are all good questions to keep in mind as I begin to challenge some of your core beliefs about sin, sexuality, marriage, nudity, lust, clothing, health, hygiene and food. Believe me, as God started to reveal His plans for me and this book, you can't imagine the thoughts and questions that entered my mind as I began to think about all the people who would likely read it – my wife, my mama, my children, my extended family, my co-workers, my pastor, and my church friends, etcetera. What will they think of this? It can be very, very difficult and downright frightening to challenge the status quo, especially with Christians who have many *well-established* but *unfounded* beliefs that the status quo is indeed *biblical,* even though they cannot tell you why or how.

"There's so much in the media telling people you have to look a certain way.... People feel so pressured that if they don't look this way they're not going to be beautiful."[2] This is probably the biggest challenge for women and young girls today, and the problem is expanding to affect our girls at a younger and younger age. "Unfortunately, it's something that society expects from women, and whoever doesn't adhere to this norm, becomes a weirdo. It makes me remember how my friends back home refer to those women (those who don't shave or wax) with disdain, with disgust. Why is it so ingrained in our culture that women have to be hair-

---

[2] Ariel Winter 2016

free in order to be 'proper' women?"[3] – Maria Garcia-Arrázola. The great hair debate is probably one of the most provocative topics that I could use to illustrate some of the issues targeted in this book. What would happen to a woman if she walked into church one Sunday morning in the western culture wearing a sleeveless blouse and having not shaved her armpits for 3 months? Oh, the shame and ridicule she would endure – maybe not in spoken words, but for sure in the minds of nearly everyone who saw her. We will address this a bit more later, but by now some of you are quite sure that I am at worst certifiably insane, and at a best a bit misguided. To that thought I would simply ask, based on what? Did God not make women with hair – yes, even the hair under their arms? On their legs? Did He, *The Creator*, get it wrong? Did it not have a purpose? Did He not say that it was "good"? Why are you or would you be offended by a lady with hairy armpits or legs? Is the best answer you can conjure be that "it's just not normal" or "nobody does that"? Would you be busy comparing her to the *real-life* Hollywood "weirdoes" who might do the same thing just for the attention? You may have never even brought such a question to mind before. Why would you? Shaving is simply a *fact* of life for a woman, right?

Your response to this by now may be – so what, generally people around me prefer that I hide certain parts of my body, dye my hair, shave my legs, wear makeup, etcetera. It makes us all feel better if we just do what's accepted and fall in line. What affect does this really have on my life or theirs? What affect does it have

---

[3] Maria Garcia-Arrázola 2016

on my husband or wife? How could an issue like this really affect the quality of my life or the lives of those I love? With her permission of course, I want to share a real-life illustration that involves my beautiful 15 year-old daughter and her relationship with me, her dad. I Love my daughter. She is beautiful! She is a unique creation in every sense of the word. She and I have a very open and loving relationship as father and daughter. However, she has recently developed two distinctly different hugs for me, her dad – one hug is what I'll call the "with-bra" hug - this is usually a good, tight, uninhibited, but normal, loving hug - and the *other* hug is a "braless" hug. This braless hug is kind of a distant, very careful, lean-in-side-ways, church-lady, I don't-want-you-touching-me-or-feeling-my-breasts-touch-you, swift, cold kind of hug. Now which one do you think I like better and why? Why do you think she is troubled about hugging her dad when there's no bra between her breasts and shirt? There's really a couple of reasons that are quite obvious in our society and church culture today. The first and most obvious reason is that we (mainly Americans and Christians) have so sexualized the female breast that young ladies (especially young Christian ladies) are hypersensitive about them – *to say the very least*. They want to be proud of them once they start to develop, but they've been taught that there must be a certain amount of shame incorporated into this as well. It's not favorable if a girl's breasts are too petite, but if they're too large or too "perky" then that's yet a completely different problem as well. For the very few young mothers who breast feed anymore, we send them into restrooms or dark corners or any possible place in order to get them away from people to do their *business*, like it's dirty and demeaning and shameful to feed their young in the way that God *certainly* intends. In the name of "modesty" we have built "nursing" rooms or "cry" rooms whereby new mothers can "discretely" go and do their "shameful" deed away from any would-be spectators. Why can't a mother sit in a church pew during a service and feed her infant in the *perfect* way that God designed? And without the assembly of a tent in order to conceal her outrageous deed? Would Jesus have asked her to step out into the hall or the restroom if he were there? Would He have asked her to leave the service at all? Would he have asked her to put a blanket over the baby's head and the mother's breast? Would it have embarrassed him to see this? Would it? You know the answer, but will you accept it? If Paul or Peter or James or John or even Jesus were to come to modern day America, would they be confined or swayed by the world in their perspective of the human body, about sexuality, about breasts and breastfeeding? Would they struggle with lust simply because Hollywood has made a pornographic cesspool of women's bodies and specifically their breasts? No! They would not be concerned at all with what man tells them about God's creation. They would not look to man to give them perspective on the human body – specifically about breasts. Any then why should you? If you would be appalled and embarrassed with a young lady very openly feeding her newborn in the middle of a church service, where did those thoughts and feelings originate? The Word or the world? You will not find such a perspective in the Word! Period. The picture of a mother nursing her young is seen over and over throughout scripture as a good, wholesome and normal – God's Normal – not the worlds. Just a very natural part of life as God intended it, nothing more. Just look what we Christians have done to it? Really what we have *allowed* the world to do to it *through* us. That is truly a shame, truly *the* shame.

It hurts me to know that my little girl cannot give me a genuine, uninhibited hug for fear that I might feel her breast squeeze up against me in the process. It hurts me to know that she feels like she has to make this discernment *every time* we hug – like I'm some stranger or weirdo who might have some lustful or lewd thought about her, should her breast press up against my body during an "authentic", braless hug. The world, Hollywood, mama, family, and to some degree the church has taught her that this is the *proper* way to hug your dad - while braless. No one sat her down and explained this to her, this came "naturally" to her as a result of the influences I just mentioned. How sad is that? So yes, the issues I will discuss can most definitely have effects that reach much farther than perhaps you've considered. Ultimately, the goal is NOT to have you hone in on a few obvious and detailed topics, but rather to have you change the way you think so that you no longer *allow* the world around you, the culture, the media, pornography, or possibly even your friends dictate how you dress, or whether you wear make-up or not, or dye your hair, or shave your legs, or even how you hug your dad!

By now you may be saying, OK, I've seen one or two of these ideas before, and perhaps you've even done some reading or study on your own already. There is certainly an overabundance of opinions and information out on the Internet, on blogs, social media or in magazines or books or seminars that speak to some degree on most of the subjects to be discussed. In fact, I will reference many of these sources as I go into detail and discuss the finer points in the chapters to follow. So why a book? My hope and my prayer is that blind eyes might be opened, and that many relationships might be strengthened or restored by the discussions that follow as a result of considering the real truth, studying God's Word and following His *true* Will. My hope is that God will be glorified as I bring to light some of those very sensitive topics that many are simply too afraid to broach. However, God knows that I would be deceiving all of you if I led you to believe that this was my only purpose or inspiration for the book. Truly, I am writing this for an audience of two, my wife and my God. If it enhances my relationship with her and glorifies Him by changing your perspective on His truth, then I will have achieved *His* goal, and the book will have been a success. I would never have sat down to write this if it were not for my dear wife and my great God. I Love you both!

His Truth Can Replace Lies

2 God's Glorious Creation

Consider for a moment all that God created - the earth, the sky, the seas, the animals, and the very intricate details of life that we are just now beginning to discover, and think about the order and the timeframe for all of this as laid out in Genesis. Though our feeble little minds are incapable of "thinking" like God, step back for just a minute and think about God's thoughts, God's Love, God's intelligence, God's vision and "intuition" when He was speaking this world into existence. (Psalms 139:17) The delicate balance of ecosystems, food-chains, vegetation, elements, weather patterns, biological processes, mathematical certainties, and man – all that must exist, not just simultaneously, but in perfect harmony and order to sustain life. Think about the very unique and intricate biophysics, cellular structure, and chemical composition of each and every living plant or animal on the planet...and we haven't even discovered all of them yet. Think about all of that with regard to His creation of man and of woman.... We get just a little glimpse into God's "thinking" in Job 38 where God is questioning Job as to where he was when He laid the foundations of the earth. He talks about making the clouds, the sea, the stars, the light, the snow, the hail, the thunderbolt and rain, and wisdom. He asked Job in verse 39, can you hunt the prey for the lion, or satisfy the appetite of the young lions when they crouch in their dens or lie in wait in their thicket? I think He is asking Job, "Do you know how to place the instincts of a lion into their being?" We mostly take for granted the instincts and behaviors of animals, especially "wild" animals, but yet God has put into every living creature a unique programming that must exist to maintain that harmony mentioned earlier. Later on in Job, He talks about the horse in chapter 39 verse 19, "did you give the horse his might? Do you clothe his neck with a mane?" In verse 27 God asks – "is it at your command that the eagle mounts up and makes his nest on high?" It becomes very apparent to Job very early into this conversation that he is, to say the least, insignificant compared to God. Yet God loves us and wants to have a relationship with us and has numbered every hair on our head. God has created everything in wisdom and with such insight and perfection that man could never even begin to understand or comprehend, let alone duplicate. We are but the part-time managers of all that He has created, and we only do that in accordance with His will and providence. We tamper with God's order at our own peril.

Imagine if you will, that if in addition to the Bible God had written a detailed handbook or two – "Life on Planet Earth" and maybe the "Working Anatomy of the Human Body" - male and female editions. Given all of the knowledge and know-how that we humans have accumulated over these thousands of years, we still have barely even scratched the surface compared to what would be contained in such books if authored by our great God! Just imagine the cure and prevention for *every* illness and disease, the secrets to *limitless* power for our "inventions", and incredible recipes for plant and animal that would literally *tickle* our taste buds. Just imagine the instructions for the ultimate sexual encounter with your spouse as illuminated by the *very* creator of our sexual bodies. Wow! That would really be incredible! This side of heaven, I don't think we'll ever completely know what would be in the pages of such books, *yet every day we strive to know*. Did you catch that? We have been slowly writing these "imaginary" books every day since the beginning of time. We search for cures, we look for more efficient and better forms of power, we look for new ideas and new ways to prepare our food and we seek to have more incredible and more pleasurable relationships with our spouses. We spend our days searching and researching and trying to understand and solve the mysteries of life. Yet, I think you would agree with me, we are nowhere close to a complete understanding of creation. We are nowhere close to completing those books. In fact, in many ways it seems that we take a few steps forward only to then fall back. On a large scale, new discoveries are made every day, and in our personal lives we see the wisdom of yesterday replaced time and time again. Unfortunately, we also discover over and over that the wisdom and convention we've passed on was not necessarily genuine.

If you review what we consider "the beginning" in the early chapters of Genesis, I believe you would agree that the first man and woman were made perfect in every way physically. Physically, God himself created us *flawless*. It's only because of sin that death and disease has kept us from ever remaining perfect here on earth. However, let us break that down and really try to see a glimpse of what God "envisioned" and the many intricate characteristics He designed into man and woman. Generally speaking, the physical human body – both male and female – is the most intricate, profound, and mysterious of all of the living things on the planet. There is nothing else like us – not even close! Even though we have made huge strides in the way of understanding the body and mind, it has been said that the more we learn, the more we realize just how much we don't know. It seems that as quickly as we learn something valuable with regard to diet or exercise or care for our bodies, we then hear something today that counters the wisdom of yesterday. For example, one day the research reports that coffee is good for you and it seems that by the end of the week they'll be another study that finds it really can be a problem. It is good to know that the science does eventually get settled on some things, but I think we have a long way to go with regard to our lifestyle choices and how they impact our longevity.

Generally speaking, it is fairly well documented that cigarette smoking has detrimental effects on most people. However, we all know someone who may have smoked several packs a day for their entire life and lived to be eighty, ninety or a hundred years old! Part of the problem with trying to understand the detailed facets of the human body is that we can all be very unique in so many ways. We do have some commonalities, but we also know that we can differ greatly in how our bodies respond to medicine or allergens, or how our diet effects our health, or even how much we can drink before we have to go pee! We are a marvelous and wonderful creation! Just think about all of the things that our bodies can do – they can heal after a broken bone or a cut, our brains can reason and control the body whether we're asleep or awake, our senses provide an incredible range of data that we use to solve problems, with the release of the hormone adrenaline we can become "super-human" and our brain along with our sensory organs are also capable of providing us intense pleasures through sight, sound, smell, taste and touch! With God's design through the gift of sex between a man and woman, we can even create a completely new life!

God built into us an amazing network of nerves and sensory organs that function in a variety of ways as we live out our lives here on earth. However, let us focus in on a few key areas and really just see how we can use them to bring pleasure, happiness and fulfillment to our lives, our marriages and the rest of our world - in abundance! All five of our senses have the capacity to bring physical and emotional pleasure to us as human beings. These pleasures can vary a little from male to female and they can certainly change as we grow from a baby to a senior adult. Also, as I had stated earlier, we are all unique and the triggers that bring us pleasure can also vary significantly from person to person, but there are many commonalities that do bring us into consistency one way or another. For example, who doesn't like to have their back scratched? I mean, it doesn't even have to be itchy, but it sure feels good for my wife to run her nails down it light and slow. How about a good back massage? Or for you ladies, I know you like a good pedicure. How about that nice hot shower when you're cold? Or how about the smell of your favorite food cooking or new born baby? For those of us in the south, how about the sound of brisk north wind as it scatters through a forest of long leaf pines on a clear, star-filled, fall night? Or the sound of the ocean waves as they crash onto the beach? What about the sight of a snow-capped mountain range across a frozen lake? The taste of your lover's lips after you're reunited from a period of separation. As I get older, just the feeling of sitting down after a long day on my feet! When we stop to consider all of the triggers that can bring us pleasure in one way or another, it should really deepen our appreciation for God and how He created us and how He Loves us.

While these every-day, simple pleasures of life are important, I really want to focus on God's ultimate pleasure gift to us through marriage. We often waste it, devalue it, and misuse it to the point where we're scared of it. So we don't talk about it - in fact we often just hide it and hide from it, pretend it's not there and of no interest to us. The world has so contorted and disfigured it, that churches won't often speak of it at all, but usually just in a negative connotation. The Christian Culture seems to just avoid it altogether, and it mostly brings anxiety to parents, and especially women, even when mentioned in a small group of believers. Because of the world's deception and misuse of it, there are many misconceptions and untruths prevailing among the Christian crowd. So much so, that many have even come to accept these deceptions as fact, even biblical. The world, Hollywood, and the media march on as they always have in an effort to misalign, misguide and ultimately destroy this *God*-created gift that is at the *very* pinnacle of all He made with regard to marriage, physical pleasure, and the human body – sex.

You could say that we are all conceived with it, at least from the perspective that we are all born either male or female with respect to our bodies. In fact, no matter how hard we try, we will never be able to intrinsically change who we are with regard to our sex, as our great God has imprinted it on every single cell in our bodies. Our basic anatomy and our attitudes about sexuality are really very similar until we hit that magical age of puberty, when our respective hormones – testosterone for boys and estrogen for girls – kick in and we transform from playful little children into a rage of emotions and feelings. Our bodies begin a transformation that results in some very dramatic changes over just a matter of a few months or years – hair begins to darken up and grow, breasts develop, voices change, menstruation starts, muscles take shape and hips widen. Emotionally, this is arguably the most vulnerable stage of human development, and yet we as parents sometimes seem to focus care and attention in all of the wrong places. This is the stage of life where we really need to figure out who we are in Christ and who we want to be as adults and future leaders, but most just follow the crowd and try not to make waves. It is at this very critical juncture in life that we need someone we trust to come along side us and be open and honest and frank with us about our bodies, about sexuality, about sex, about sin and what God really expects of us. Very few of us have received that kind of support growing up, and to be honest, I don't know that I've done a great job as a parent of providing it either. Sometimes as parents we passively decide that conversation about these issues could only bring more interest, which will only bring exploration, and ultimately lead our children into sin. Well, I think you'll agree that NOT being proactive, open and honest about it hasn't exactly worked out very well either. If we do not instill in our children a healthy view of sex, sexuality and marriage, then the world will certainly fill them with lies. We'll peer a little deeper into this a little later, but for now let's just agree that we are aware of the issues and we know that there is likely a better way.

It has been established that while we are all more similar than we are different, we also know that each one of us can be unique in some ways as well. While that may sound a little contradictory, let me explain. While I believe that God wove into most men and women a craving for sexual pleasure and exploration, we also know that this is not true of each and every person. In fact, we can know that this is not the case, as Paul in 1 Corinthians 7:8-9 implies that there would be some who could exercise self-control, and would simply not have an interest or an appetite for sexual intimacy. Paul urges those who can, to abstain from marriage, and thus from sexual intimacy. For most of the rest of our discussion with regard to sexuality, the focus will be on that group of people who *do* crave sexual intimacy, who *do* need a partner, and who *do* have sexual desire and passion for sexual pleasure and emotional connection.

The Bible says that God created woman *specifically* for man. (Gen 1:18; 1 Cor 11:9) Specifically. In fact, He goes so far as to say that it was not good for Adam to be alone. This was the first mention in Genesis of something that God saw as "not good". So right away in the Word we see a specific need for sex, intimacy, pleasure and companionship, and we see God provide a *specific* solution to this deficiency, the woman. It has been implied by Paul H. Byerly[4] (a popular Christian sexuality blogger) that perhaps even God knew that He could not meet all of man's needs *directly* and so he provided for Adam indirectly by creating the woman.

---

[4] Paul H. Byerly 2011 – The Generous Husband

The bible says that woman was created specifically to be a perfect companion or a "help meet" for the man, and God specifically commanded them to be fruitful and multiply and fill the earth. In fact, this was perhaps the first command that God gave to them as a couple and as people. God is commanding them to engage in sexual activity and to keep at it, and no doubt to enjoy it along the way! Dr. R. Albert Mohler, president of the Southern Baptist Theological Seminary, says that sexual pleasure is not an *accident* of human biology – it is one of the Creator's sweetest gifts to human beings. The promise of sexual pleasure and satisfaction is to draw us into the marital covenant, and then shared joy of physical union is a *vital* part of the marital bond.[5] In addition to multiplying, the only other command that we see mentioned for Adam and Eve was that they were to refrain from eating of the fruit of the tree of knowledge of good and evil. Of course, we know what happened beyond that, and then we have the rest of the bible that tells us the history of God and man and ultimately of Jesus. However, I want to bring your attention to something, really to the time prior to sin and the fall, but just after God had created Adam and Eve. So far as we know by the Word of God, there were no other constraints or limitations or commands given to this first couple beyond those we've already mentioned. Ponder this for a minute.... here they are in a perfect garden, nude (though they didn't know it, it had not been defined yet), alone, and free to do most anything they

---

[5] Dr. R. Albert Mohler Jr. 2004 -
http://www.albertmohler.com/2004/03/25/the-bible-on-sex-the-way-to-happiness-and-holiness/

please, with that one exception of eating of the tree of the knowledge of good and evil. If you or I could go change places with them right this minute, would you really want to go? It would be frightening and uncomfortable for many of you, to say the least. For those of you who would be honest enough to admit that you would probably be uncomfortable, embarrassed or apprehensive, do you even see the problem with that? Read the next sentence and then put down the book for a minute, find a quiet place, and close your eyes. If you are married, think about you and your spouse, nude, alone in a perfect garden, perfect weather, perfect food, a *God-perfect* environment.... no kids, no people, no church, no pastors, no police, no judges, no culture, no society, no "normal", no "abnormal", no past, no parents, no previous partners, no worries, no shame, no guilt, no baggage... I think this ideal is what God *wants* for each of our marriages, but how incredibly difficult it is for us to even get close to it in the 21st century. How many of these burdens and worries and inhibitions do *we* maintain in our marriage *unnecessarily*? This is the one area of our lives that God has given us *complete* freedom and yet many of you *choose* to be bound. This is the one pleasure of sight, sound, smell, taste and touch upon which God has placed the *least* amount of restriction in terms of indulgence and enjoyment, and yet remains one of the *most* problematic issues within marriage today. Why?

There's a lot of debate out there with regard to what's right and what's wrong in terms of sexual boundaries according to the Bible. With just the first few chapters of Genesis we can dismiss a good bit of that misinformation and clarify the rest. We know that God created man and woman and the woman was designed to be the wife (i.e. sexual partner, help meet, lover) of man. God created the woman specifically to meet the very particular sexual needs of the man in every conceivable way. So man was not to be the wife of man, nor was woman to be the husband of woman. At this point in the world and in the relationship of Adam and Eve, we can safely assume that ALL forms of sexual intimacy were on the table, and they were free to enjoy whatever they wanted to do with, or to, one another. That's pretty straightforward, right? Also, pretty frightening for some of you. So French kissing was good. So necking was good. So oral sex was good. So masturbation was good. So mutual masturbation was good. All sexual positions were good – sitting, standing, lying, front, back... as much as they wanted with as many variations as they pleased – let your *married* imagination run for a minute with your spouse (for those of you who can) – it was all good – for a man and a woman in a marriage relationship – *it IS still all good*. Because of the world's perversion of God's creation, this will be very difficult, if not impossible, for some of you to comprehend. So from a sin perspective, *anything* they wanted to do with one another was good, God said so. We have nothing to indicate that Adam and Eve had *any* inhibitions about doing anything that brought pleasure to one another. In fact, I can imagine that they we're actively and enthusiastically exploring one another and trying to figure out what felt good. We can also assume that Adam likely had a beard and hair in all of the *normal* places on his body and Eve most certainly had hairy armpits and legs and mons, and *yet*, they were *emphatically* attracted to one another (very counter to our current culture). I mention this because in most every depiction you and I have ever seen, we find Adam clean shaven and Eve's only hair on the top of her head. This was certainly *not* accurate for either of them, unless we also assume that they were created as prepubescent male and female people, which from what the Bible says does not appear to be the case. From a sexual and relational point of view, they were purely, completely and perfectly free... free from any cultural or societal norms, free from sexual inhibition, free from manufactured beauty, free from tradition, free from shame, free from lust, free from peer pressure, free from opinions and ridicule and free from sin.

Obviously, we no longer live in a sin-free world, but there is nothing in God's Word that would indicate that He does not want us to have a married relationship *just like this* with our spouse *today*. We can still be free from *all* of those things I mentioned, except sin. If you are disgusted or appalled with the picture that I just painted in the previous paragraph, keep in mind that this was God's painting, not mine. As a matter of fact, given the details of the Song of Solomon, we have all the latitude we need as married heterosexual couples to live it up when it comes to our sexual desires. There is NO condemnation of any sort with regard to the sexual relationship of a married man and woman. Why in the world are we so content to be so inhibited? Why are we so quiet about our sexuality? Why aren't we celebrating our sexual freedom in marriage in Christ every chance we get? The bible says in Philippians 4:8 that whatever is true, whatever is honorable, whatever is just, whatever is pure, whatever is lovely, whatever is commendable, if there is any excellence, if there is anything worthy of praise, *think about these things*. Are we given any reason anywhere in scripture to think that our married sexual relationship does not fit into God's "whatever"? Is your sexual relationship with your spouse worthy of praise? Have you ever even asked yourself that question? Is there a possibility that so many people are seeking sexual fulfilment in *other* ways (pornography, homosexuality, transgenderism, pedophilia, bestiality, adultery, incest, etc.) in part because they look at Christian marriages and right away they see no satisfaction or excitement in our sexuality – yet they yearn for it? For the most part, the world sees us as a very sexually repressed people. Should that really be the case? *Did God put sexuality into our being expecting us to live repressed and inhibited?* If you think so, why? Recently our Sunday school class (of married couples) was asked what Old Testament book they would like to study? Just the mention of Song of Solomon was enough to make people blush and speak out *against* it. What reasons do we give the lost world to *want* to be in a heterosexual relationship, married to one person, and remain there for the rest of their lives? We Christians don't even *want* to study God's very Word on the subject!

From what I read online and see and experience in my own life with family, friends and acquaintances, there is a definite lack of sexual fulfilment in marriages today. It has been the number one primary or underlying cause for divorce as far back as I can find data. You probably won't find many divorced couples who would say that their sex life was incredible, but they still sought divorce. Many non-Christians see this and make the logical decision to live together and "try out" a relationship before making the commitment to marriage, and who can really blame them? They see the turmoil and rate of divorce or they have experienced divorce first hand and just choose to avoid the risk by living together. Many Christians know the frustration of a married "Christian" sex-life and they see divorce as an option but are very reluctant to re-marry for the same reasons. If the married Christian is in a sexually repressed relationship and chooses to "honor" the commitment no matter what the cost, then *what kind of married example is this for either the lost or the saved?* How can we continue to tell our young people about how wonderful marriage is and how serious the commitment *should* be when they look around and see divorce and sexual frustration? Why are we Christians somehow afraid to say that sex is important in a marriage? I would draw a lot of fire from most pastors and Christians if I were to say that sex is the *most* important element. Is this somehow contrary to scripture? If an abundant sexual relationship is imperative to a great marriage, (and we know that it is) then we must start living this out in our marriages to be a *witness* to the lost world and our own children. I don't think that this can happen if 100% of our *sexual* relationship happens behind a closed and locked bedroom door with the lights off, nor am I advocating that we "live-stream" all of the intimate details of each of our love making details to the world. However, much like Julie Siebert[6] says in a quote I will use in Chapter 4, our sexuality and the intimacy that we share with our spouse must be *evident* throughout every day of our lives. As good "Church" people, we've gotten so pious

---

[6] Julie Siebert – intimacyinmarriage.com

that a little pat on the "booty" or a little sexual flirtation between a husband and a wife in a public setting is more than frowned upon, it's downright *immoral*. My wife and I have had this discussion with regard to our home and our children when it comes to how much affection is too much for their eyes and understanding. The question comes up, well what are we teaching our kids when they see dad pat mom's bottom or squeeze her breast? What if we teach them (by living it out) that mom and dad love to flirt, kiss, admire, and touch one another, and we enjoy doing so *within* and *because* we are married. Teach them that God not only *approves* of this, but He says that it is *good*. This behavior is expected *only* because we are married and bound to one another for the rest of our lives. If this is our answer to our children when questioned, not only will it keep *them* from patting mom's behind, but it will also follow them into adulthood so that they understand sex is not only reserved for marriage, it can be *expected to be abundant!* The most important impact this will have on them is that they will have a much better appreciation for the intimate relationship that exists between their parents. In a world where sexual partners come and go and divorce is all around us, this will leave a huge impression on their thoughts on the validity of marriage and the covenant relationship that they will establish with their spouse later in life.

3 Trouble

As Christians, we understand that as a result of sin entering the world, man was corrupted and separated from God. At the point where man sinned, God intervened and ultimately placed man under the law beyond the commands that were issued at the garden. Most, if not all, of the commands given in the Old Testament served to protect people from discord or disease or ensure their future in one way or another as they pursued the abundant life in a fallen world. Specifically, most of the references to sex, marriage, or pleasure really provide a guide for what God intended to be the family unit. Most of the restrictive law in the Old Testament with regard to sex really focused on situations and issues that were outside of the marriage relationship between a man and a woman – or at least should be! There are very few references in the law with regard to the sexual relationship between a married man and woman, but in the New Testament Paul goes into some detail regarding marriage and the roles of the husband and wife. Ephesians 5:22-33 and 1 Peter 3:1-7 lay out some specific instructions with regard to each and how we should conduct ourselves within the marriage relationship. As I referenced in Chapter 2, 1 Corinthians chapter 7 goes into a bit more detail with regard to marriage, divorce and sex. There are many other New Testament references to marriage and sex in Matthew, Mark, Luke, Romans, Galatians, Colossians, I Timothy, Hebrews and Revelation. In 1 Corinthians Paul suggests that the husband and wife should agree upon and set aside some time from their sexual appetites in order to pray. This is the *only* prohibition that I can find in the New Testament with specific regard to the sexual desires and appetites of the *married* couple. One. This implies that we could, or we should, be engaged in sexual oneness with our spouse *most* of the time, just taking a little break here and there to pray as necessary (lighten up, I'm just kidding - maybe). So as we looked at Adam and Eve in the last chapter and the sexual freedom that they enjoyed with one another, we see that same freedom extended to the married man and woman in the New Testament world as well. Again, there are very few (really only one) prohibitions on the sexual relationship of the married couple.

The predominant sin problem that either spouse faces within a marriage with regard to sex stems from a lustful desire to have an adulterous relationship with anyone who is not their spouse. Probably the most well-known example of this in the Bible is when David sent for Bathsheba and had her brought to him so that he could fulfill his desire to have sex with her in 2 Samuel 11. Notice that I did not say the problem was when David "saw" Bathsheba bathing from the roof (the temptation), nor was the problem even David's admiration of her nude and beautiful body. As many of the old testament laws and even Jesus' mention of lust in Matthew 5:28 indicate (Matt 5:28 - But I say to you that everyone who looks at a woman with lustful intent has already committed adultery with her in his heart.), it's not the looking or even the delight of a woman's beauty and body that gets us into trouble, it is the coveting. Lust is most always a "secret" sin insomuch as no one but you and God may ever know if, or when, you have lusted. It's not like murder or rape or theft in that you can lust in your mind and heart and the outside world can appear to be unaffected, perhaps for a little while. Jason Staples[7], a professor in Religious Studies at the University of North Carolina at Chapel Hill, goes into great detail with regard to the scripture and how the churches and *some* pastors have misinterpreted Matthew 5:28. He goes on to say that their ideas are "flat wrong" and really lead into some harmful consequences with regard to our society and teaching our children. Staples lists this verse as being the number one misinterpreted Bible verse in all of scripture, and he really lays out the standard for truth and understanding of what Jesus *was* saying, and what he wasn't. *As there are numerous pastors, authors and blogs that explore this topic and verse and come to the same conclusion,* I encourage you to study this for yourself and see what you ascertain. On the flipside of this, there is the argument that women are really somewhat to blame for the lustful stares of men, and that they should police their clothing in order that they might not cause their brother to sin. Arguments are made today that go so far as to blame rape on the woman's choice of apparel and completely vindicate the man's role in the crime. Let me be sure to tell you now that I do NOT support this whatsoever. Just like David, a man *is* responsible for his own actions and his own thoughts, *no matter what temptations come before him*. James 1:14 says that each person is tempted when he is lured and enticed by his own sinful desire. With respect to the subject of women and their apparel, here's where the second most misinterpreted verse comes into play, 1 Timothy 2:9 – "In

---

[7] Jason Staples – www.jasonstaples.com 2016

like manner also, that women adorn themselves in modest apparel, with shamefacedness and sobriety; not with braided hair, or gold, or pearls, or costly array". Most people today immediately think of the word modest in this verse as referencing the coverage or fit or sexual nature of the clothing that is worn by a woman. As Rachel Held Evans explains in her article - "Modesty: I Don't Think it Means What you Think it Means", the reality is that the word modest here does not refer to sexuality, nudity or how much skin is showing, but rather materialism. The writers of the Old and New Testament were concerned about people flaunting their wealth by wearing expensive clothes and jewelry while others suffered in poverty. As Rachel says in her article, "biblical modesty isn't about managing the sexual impulses of other people; it's about cultivating humility, propriety and deference within ourselves". At the time Paul wrote this, and even in our modern world, we often see clothing as one of the factors that separate the rich from the poor. Sometimes this can be seen literally in third world countries where the poor are naked for the simple reason that they cannot afford clothes. However, in the United States we often see this in the form of "high-society" brands that divide those who shop at K-mart from those who can afford Macy's. "It's important not to turn the worship service into a beauty pageant, because women would spend all their time competing and none of it worshiping. It can send the poor women home in tears and puff the rich women up with pride, and this is not supposed to be the outcome of Christian worship." – Ken Collins[8]

It seems that the misinterpretation of this verse is one that causes women the most angst and has somewhat created such a divide in our current Christian culture. The mention of braided hair, gold, pearls and costly attire seems to be dismissed entirely by the Christian community because these things were simply "cultural" for the day and they aren't relevant in our modern American society – *or are they?* The problem with that reasoning is that you then must also dismiss the misinterpretation about respectable attire and modesty if you are willing to overlook the other details of the verse. In Christian circles, we hear a lot about people "cherry-picking" the Bible to make it fit their own agendas or give reprieve from their sin and lifestyles. Most of us would agree that we must accept and build our lives upon the *complete* Word of God, not just the parts that make us feel good or fit neatly into our particular ideals. Entire weekends and conferences are dedicated and based solely on that one word – modesty. The rest of the verse is never discussed. Much less the many other verses regarding a woman's appearance. (1 Peter 3:3; 3:5; 2 Cor. 5:12) Yet we certainly "cherry-pick" this verse just to suit our modern cultural agenda, when we should either take the *entire* verse at face value or dismiss it completely, based on our current American Western way of life. If we follow the verse and apply it *completely* to our current culture, then shouldn't we really examine ourselves (especially women) to be sure

---

[8] Ken Collins – 2017 -
http://www.kencollins.com/answers/question-31.htm

that we are truly pursuing *genuine* biblical modesty? If we looked carefully at this *whole* verse, I think we would be surprised and dismayed at what we would find with regard to our modern, western, church culture.

I hope by now that you've taken the time to put down this book and study some scripture for yourselves by consulting several different translations, commentaries, or maybe even looking into some of the Greek or Hebrew words from the original text. While I believe that a portion of the sexual anxiety and deviance in our world today is a result of how the church and believers have misconstrued scripture, I also understand that it was never God's intention for sexual experimentation or satisfaction outside of the marriage. For a young man to have sexual urges and to gaze at the beauty of a woman – yes, even her "private parts"- is not sin. By the same token, for a beautiful lady to wear revealing clothing or even to be completely nude in the presence of a man is not automatically sin. However, with the wrong timing and with the wrong motivations, either of these situations could certainly still be wrong. It's all about the heart. It's all about the intentions. However, don't take my word for it, as the Word says in 1 Thessalonians 5:21, you should convince yourself of this by a *careful* test and study of the Word. Will you take the time to do that? The problem has been that we as a society and as Christians very rarely apply Thessalonians 5:21 or Romans 12:2 – we do not test or examine anything, we just go with the flow. Once again, if we would just take God at His word, we find instruction and help when we need it. In the next couple of chapters, we'll take a detailed look at each of these scenarios to see how they can possibly be genuine. After all, you've been taught, really indoctrinated, as women that you should dress "modestly" and cover up your *sexual* selves, and we've been told as men that we should not look upon a lady who is not our wife – *especially* if she is nude!

4 The Look

Oh how we all marvel at a spectacular sunrise or sunset. Especially if it is painted over a body of water or with a snowcapped mountain in the foreground, with just a few delicate clouds to light up the sky in hues of bright oranges, reds and yellows! While I believe that each of us have some individually unique ideas about beauty with regard to the world around us, I also believe that most of us share an inalienable appreciation for many of the same spectacles in God's glorious creation. In Romans 1 verse 20 Paul states "For His invisible attributes, namely, his eternal power and divine nature, have been clearly perceived, ever since the creation of the world, in the things that have been made". Whether that's a sunrise or a snow-covered mountain range or a pristine white sandy beach on a clear blue ocean, there are many, many sites around the world that amaze us and fill us with His joy and wonder. "The human body is beautiful in all the same ways as anything is beautiful." – Brent Leggett.[9] I would add to what Brent has stated and say that in many ways the human body – specifically the female human body – is more beautiful than most anything else on the planet. So, His invisible attributes, namely, His eternal power and divine nature, have been clearly perceived, ever since the creation of the world, *in the female human body*. Does this disturb you? Is the female human body not included in the things that the Father has created? Maybe you've been blinded by the

---

[9] Brent Leggett - http://flashme.com.au/brentsblog/category/lust-beauty-and-freedom/

world and perhaps the church from ever seeing this scripture in *that* light. The sexual immorality and abuse of the female form has so overwhelmed your senses that you cannot see clearly. When it comes to a desire or compulsion to appreciate or gaze at the human body, for the most part it *seems* that men's inclination to look at women is far more prevalent than is the opposite – *or so we've been programmed*. In this perverted world, one thing that is lacking in our Christian worldview is a healthy perspective of sexual beauty *apart* from lust and immorality. This hasn't always been true. To say that a man could look upon a female, especially a nude female, and see and appreciate the same beauty as he does in a sunset is preposterous to most. In fact, most women automatically assume that all men are irrational perverts, and most men do not *understand* that they can choose to separate the beauty of a woman from their own lust and desire, *nor have they ever even tried*. In both cases, we have been *programmed and trained* to act and feel this way by the lost world, and to some degree the church. Do you think David was the *only* one to ever see Bathsheba from the rooftop taking a bath? Do you think that this was the *first and only* time she had ever been out there bathing? Do you think that he was the only one to *ever* see her nude besides her husband? If you do a little research, you'll find that outdoor bathing was quite common for this time period. Most people couldn't afford to even have a facility at home, they relied on the rivers and lakes or government established facilities for bathing. Historians tell us that bathing was done very openly for the most part in rivers or lakes, as was the washing of garments. For the sake of our discussion, we will refer exclusively to natural, heterosexual people and we can assume that principles discussed will apply uniformly for both the male and the female. Not that a female can't have an appreciation for the beauty of another female, but for a heterosexual Christian that admiration would be completely devoid of any sexual inclination or desire for the female body, as would the male for a male body. For the sake of this discussion, we will only examine that natural, Godly, heterosexual response, as it will play a significant role in how we understand the joy and wonder of the anatomy of the opposite sex.

As we grow from toddlers to young children and into adolescence, we begin to recognize that boys and girls are different from one another - very different. Albeit we make this distinction primarily due to external or artificial indicators applied by parents such as clothing, toys, hair styles, activities and to some degree our interests. I dare say that for some period of time leading into adolescence, it could be very hard to distinguish a male from a female (apart from seeing their genitals) if we were to accurately duplicate these "external" elements for any given male or female child. There's really nothing visually about the *clothed* body of a prepubescent human that definitively defines their sex. As was mentioned in Chapter 2, we all undergo this incredible transformation during puberty, and in just a matter of a couple of years there is usually *quite* a distinction that can be made with regard to the sex of a person – clothed or not. It's really during this time of our lives that we begin to notice those real distinctions in the male and female form. Admittedly, it is also during this time that we guys begin to appreciate the beauty and wander into the fascination of the female and experience the joy and wonder of looking at her, as well as deal with the consequences of being attracted to her. Although, here in America the wonder of this has really become somewhat of an *artificial* idea. Let me explain...

In America, as mentioned already, our "modesty" has so over-sexualized women and their bodies that we force mothers into restrooms to breastfeed their babies. Think about that for a minute... Our infatuation, and really our apprehensive attitude with regard to breasts and nipples, has driven us to the point where mothers must take their newborn babies into the *same* rooms where we defecate and urinate in order to feed them. No part of that is right or moral or biblical! On the other hand, we have Hollywood and the media and now the Internet that feed us a constant stream of teasers and sexually provocative headlines so that our obsession and reservations will grow even *more* out of control. The stream of artificial reality further complicates matters as most of the images of women or men that we see in media are sporting plastic surgery, dyed hair and gobs of makeup - in *addition* to the digital image enhancements. With digital imaging and "fashion technology", there really isn't anything about a person's body that cannot be hidden or enhanced as desired in just a matter of minutes, and we can do all of this from our phones!

Going back to the breasts, there are many countries today where women are completely topless every day and it is considered completely *normal* by both the women and the men of that society. There are some developing countries and Pacific Islands and places in Africa where the women *were* topless for hundreds if not thousands of years until the arrival of

Christian missionaries who *taught* them that they were "immodest". To be fair, there have also been some countries that were topless until the arrival and spread of the Muslim religion as well. The reason why I call America's infatuation with breasts (and really our children's fascination with nudity) artificial is because we have introduced and enabled the problem. Hollywood and the media do more and more every day to provoke the "Christian Right" with blatant – in your face - sexual propaganda, and the Christians simply stack the deck and prescribe even more "modesty" and shame with regard to our bodies and human sexuality. The churches and the parents' method for "controlling" sexual urges in young people has been a lot of guilt and shame mixed with very little open discussion about the body, sexuality and Jesus. Our association of nudity with lust has created this firestorm between the religions and the world whereby both sides are in a constant battle for the minds of each other. Both of these agendas make life more and more problematic for our young Christian men and women while at the same time promoting sexual promiscuity out in the secular side of the world. The campaigns are both building, but I believe that both the lost and the saved are paying a high price for holding their ground. We are allowing the world to steal something from us that God created *especially* for us to enjoy and pursue in marriage, and the sad part of it is that most of us don't even see it happening. We're blind. (Luke 6:39) Pastor David Hatton writes "Far from honoring the human body and its gender distinctions as sacred ground, we've religiously depicted them as avenues of temptation and lust. Our confident legalisms and manmade scruples to *insure* purity and morality have basically pornified the body! By redefining our physical forms and our sex organs as obscenities, we've paved the way for pornographers to defile that which was meant to be part of our Trinitarian Maker's Self-portrait. With a prudish brush we've painted a lewd image of the sexuality through which God intended to proclaim His message of redemption. If this theological error is not sin, then missing the mark has lost its meaning!"[10]

Take my now eight year-old son for instance, he's not interested in the slightest bit in his mother's breasts or butt or genitals. If she's around him nude (and this does still occur), he doesn't acknowledge it at all. It's not until we (and the world) indoctrinate him with the shame of the human body that his perspective will change. It's not until we *establish* the taboo of the nude female body, or just simple nudity in general, that our kids begin to react. By now my 17 year-old is very careful that he doesn't see too much of either of his parents as he is "grossed-out" by too much skin! How did he get this way – by the world or the Word? I know it's a bit of an extreme example, but this is exactly what has happened to most of the western world. I recall a statement made by Julie Siebert of the intimacyinmarriage.com website[11], "When healthy sexual intimacy is so woven into the fabric of how we do life, then we barely notice it as a separate entity. When it's not, then it's a constant problem". From all of my study, she's exactly right! But I think this same statement could hold true with regard to

---

[10] David Hatton – 2012 -
http://pastordavidrn.blogspot.com/2012_07_01_archive.html
[11] Julie Siebert – intimacyinmarriage.com

simple nudity in some settings as well. The problem with nudity in the United States is that most people are either in one ditch or another when it comes to healthy sexuality. The media, Hollywood and the music industry glamourize infidelity, adultery, homosexuality and more while the church and the Christians continue to condemn and teach their children all of the "do nots" of sexuality with none of the *good* that God intended. We tell the world and our children about all of the things we are against, without telling them about any of the wonderful things that we should be for. Our sexuality is a part of everyday life for each of us, whether we want it to be or not – there's nothing we can do about it. *God wove it into our being and He called it good.* However, we must decide how we live with it - whether we ignore it, we embrace it, we like it, we hate it, or we make the most abundant life we can of it. I'm not saying that we should ever *plan* to have open intercourse with our spouse right in front of the eight-year-old, but what I am saying is that we shouldn't view this as something to scar them for life if they happened to catch us by accident late one night in the bedroom. I can only speak with regard to one woman on this topic, but I have read a lot of blogs and comments from women, and most are way too uptight about their sexuality in view of their kids. Have you ever stopped to consider that some sexual flirtation and play between a husband and wife in front of their *own* children may actually be healthy and even beneficial to them? Have you ever considered how families back in Jesus' day lived, many times in a single-room tent or hut? Have you ever considered the families from just a few hundred years ago who lived all together in a tiny single-room log farm house? As my wife and I recently visited some of these old, log, one-room homes, I thought about how many kids were raised in many of those households. Much of the time a dozen children from the age of birth to probably 18 years old were likely in the same room when each of their younger siblings were conceived. (Perhaps you haven't thought much about that before.) It *was* perfectly normal. If we had to do that now days, none of us would have any kids! How about the sexual escapades of Solomon and his lover in the garden for the world to see? From my experience with my own children, I think we do a lot more damage than good when we make such a taboo out of healthy, normal, *married* sexuality, or even simple nudity between a husband and wife, even when in eyesight of the children. If we could somehow normalize married sexuality, do you think the world's perverted agenda could thrive like it does?

So here's the question we're all wanting to have answered (or the question that most of you have already *inaccurately* answered in your minds): is it wrong for the Christian to either view nudity or be nude in the presence of someone who is not their spouse? My seemingly vague answer to this is a firm – it depends! Ecclesiastes 3:1 says for everything there is a season, and a time for every matter under heaven. Am I seemingly giving you the reader a reason or justification to dive off into pornography and lust? (Like I could anyway) Absolutely NOT! Quite the opposite in fact. In my study of the subject on blogs and reports and books and sermons and conversations with friends and the Word, *my* conclusion is that it varies depending on the event, the people involved, and the timing. I'm not trying to rationalize sin or say that we should purposefully flirt with temptation, or say that you should go out and look for nudity or reasons to be nude in front of others, but I am hoping that you will dig a little deeper into the subject and make your own reasonable decisions based on the Word and *unbiased* reason. (Remember, neither I nor God are responsible for this being such a big deal.) I think you will find the same variance in the Bible as there were times when God *commanded* the nudity of His prophets (Isaiah 20:2, 1 Samuel 19:24), as well as many times when it was viewed as shameful. For example, we accept it as completely necessary and normal for a person to be nude in front of their doctor, and for the doctor to see scores of nude people in his daily practice. Not only just to see the nudity of both sexes, but to touch and squeeze and to *intimately* examine the very intricate details of their most "private" anatomy. Along those lines, there are more male nurses practicing than ever before in our history. They see nude women of all ages, shapes and sizes, races and religions on a daily basis, and neither we nor they think much of it, really (or at least we shouldn't). Of course, until recently we really haven't ever given much thought to all of the female nurses out there with regard to their care for male patients over the years. So are all of those doctors and nurses just practicing sin on a daily basis, or do they have some special permission from God because they are healthcare workers? Are all of these people looking with lust or sexual desire on each and every patient they encounter? Is it possible to *intimately* examine the "sexual" organs of a person and not lust? Or could it be that because of the pressures and sin of the world that we have applied a lot of unnecessary and unbiblical scrutiny to something that should be, or at least could be, *perfectly* normal? In Acts chapter 10, Peter describes a dream that he had about clean and unclean animals. The scripture says that God told him to kill and eat, but Peter was disgusted by the notion of eating and "unclean" animal. God's people had not eaten of these animals for thousands of years, if ever at all, by this time. Look at God's response to Peter's disgust at the notion of eating the unclean animals – "do not call what God has made clean unclean". Has man called anything unclean today that God has made clean or that He never called unclean? Are we allowing the world and the traditions of men to taint our view of the human body? Did God ever even suggest that a bare female breast was impure or perverted or lewd?

David Hatton, a pastor who was also a registered labor and delivery nurse for some 30 years, has this to say about our western culture – "Through an intense pattern of cultural and religious training, we are blinded from seeing nudity as anything but a lewd sexual display. This blindness insulates us from the fact that, for most of human history, the sight of the naked body was a very common occurrence that did not draw undue attention or automatically create erotic excitement. But modern attention has been so captivated by society's sexualization of the body that this obsession has become an earmark of Western civilization. Sadly, most who grow up indoctrinated with such a mental image of the body are blinded from seeing how this view misshapes human thinking. But experience has forced many normal people to acknowledge the devastating influence of this abnormal focus on their minds and lives."[12] We have ultimately learned and taught our children a shameful view of the body, and it has only served to advance the agenda of the lost world. We have ultimately played a role in the creation and perpetuation of pornography in so much as we continue to justify it by teaching this shame to generation after generation. Just think back to my eight year-old for a minute, let's extrapolate his current, innocent view of his mom's nude female body out a few years down the road into puberty. If it were possible to isolate him from the influences of the world (and the church), *when would he change his mind about his mom's body?* Will he just wake up one day and decide that his mom's nudity is a big deal? Is lewd? Is pornographic? Immoral? If he isn't taught a perverted, shameful, solely sexual view of the body, then he is far less likely to ever look at a woman (clothed or nude) and see her as a sexual object. And isn't that what we all want? If he doesn't even acknowledge that she's sexually provocative by simply being nude, how could he possibly have sexual thoughts about her or lust after her? David Hatton[13] elaborates on this very topic in his blog and in the books he's authored. I would encourage you to go to his site and look at the years of experience he has and the biblical reasoning for the ideas which are really just God's design for us. If seeing the nude human body is a sin, many would then argue that being a doctor, or nurse or any healthcare professional gives one a license to view nudity without sin. Think about that for a minute... It becomes very difficult for man to draw

---

[12] David Hatton -
http://pastordavidrn.homestead.com/files/rebuilding-links.html
[13] David Hatton – pastordavidrn.blogspot.com

those hard lines with regard to nudity and sin when it comes to healthcare or art or massage therapy and many other areas of daily living. The bible does not condemn with regard to simple nudity, but yet man has created a lot of rules that we Christians must live by in order to be free from this "sin". Rules that are so ingrained in our society and minds that we don't even question their validity with regard to the Word. *What does God think about our disregard for His truth?* Do you think a doctor or nurse *looks* at nudity in the same way the rest of the world does? Do you have a family member or close friend who is a doctor or nurse or works in healthcare in some way? I would encourage you to go have a frank discussion with them regarding their views of the human body and how they *view* simple nudity and sexuality. I'm not asking you to just blindly trust anything someone may write in a book or a blog or preach from a pulpit, but rather get out there and do some unbiased research on your own and see what conclusions you draw. Get into God's Word, listen to what He reveals to you about the subject, and try to stay objective about your conclusions by *not letting this perverted world influence you.* Here's what Brent Leggett, an Australian Photographer with an advanced degree in theology has to say with regard to the current culture there–

> "We have lived with such a state of paranoia about causing others to stumble that we have grown up a generation of morally oversensitive Christians. This is not to cast the blame onto the shoulders of wives and women. We are all suffering under a condition that is fueled by an unchecked sexual and visual feast on the media's

part, a complete and uncritical prohibition on the church's part, and a series of subsequent misconceptions that we carry as individuals about ourselves and members of the opposite sex. The chief casualty is marriages. Relational dysfunction, caused by lack of trust, brings sexual dissatisfaction to an all-time high. This solidifies a state wherein men are more prone to sexualize the beauty of other women, their wives become defensive and critical and both parties become deeply disconnected emotionally."[14]

...And as a result, we suffer a high rate of divorce – "The chief casualty is marriages." I hope that hits you like a proverbial 2x4 upside the head Christian friend. I hope you take offense to that – not from me, but from the Word of God. (Malachi 2:16) Now I understand that the church and the Word of God should, and definitely do, have a say when it comes to the Christian woman, but if each person and each culture defines what "modesty" is and is not, then the only possible solution to the problem is to cover our bodies entirely from head to toe no matter where you live. However, as stated before, so much of what the church proclaims as truth in this area is based entirely on tradition and culture and *not* the Word of God. The Word says that we should be careful not to add to nor take away from the Holy Bible. Yet look at what we saw with the Pharisees do back in Jesus' day, and I know that we see some of it now with regard to how we convey sexuality to our youth. For example, in

---

[14] Brent Leggett – Brent's blog
http://flashme.com.au/brentsblog/curriculum-vitae/2016

my life I have chosen to abstain almost completely from alcohol consumption, as I see the degrading and sometimes even life threatening affects it can have on a person. Like I have personally chosen to do with alcohol, Christianity by and large has *taught* our youth to just abstain completely from any hint of sexuality altogether, rather than convey to them both the pleasures and the pitfalls of our human bodies. While this may be fine for *my* choice with regard to alcohol consumption, I totally disagree with it for the teachings of sexuality, beauty, and the human body. Alcohol consumption is entirely avoidable, sexuality is certainly not. So wouldn't this lead our young men down a wrong path into sexual exploration and curiosity? Wouldn't it make the women even more vulnerable to sexual attacks and harassment? Wouldn't this lead to promiscuity and sex and ultimately children out of wedlock? Absolutely not. No more than McDonald's commercials lead vulnerable people into obesity or banks lead thieves into a life of crime. Women aren't raped more often at the beach, even though much more revealing clothing is worn while there. At some point with regard to all sin and crime, we have to place the blame on the heart of the person. God's Word says in James 1:14 "But each person is tempted when he is lured and enticed by his own desire." As we have seen in recent days with regard to murder and gun-control, the problem is not the weapon or location or even the victim. The problem lies within the heart of the murderer. People have recently used knives, ropes, trucks, cars, airplanes, and even their own fists to murder other people. Removing all of those items from society won't greatly affect the rate of murder because the murderer is going to kill no matter what. A group of young men in an art class gazing at a nude female model as they paint her are no more apt to sexually assault her just because they've *seen* her body. They are likely more apt to respect and appreciate her for the beauty and strength she bestows into their life by becoming more vulnerable to them. If more men and boys had respect and appreciation for women in this way – especially the normal, un-retouched, non-digitally enhanced women, nude or clothed – do you really think that the pornography industry could stay in business? If every day, "normal" nudity had not been made into this huge taboo, if we had not been brainwashed from such an early age to see the human body *exclusively* as a lewd, lustful, sexual, immoral, as an overpowering temptation, if we had not been taught to be *ashamed* of our bodies from such an early age, then how could the cheap, dirty, deceitfulness of the pornography industry possibly thrive or even survive? If "modesty" is not cultural, then the same standard should exist from the church's perspective around the world. If it is cultural, then wouldn't that make God a hypocrite? If there is a standard in terms of how much skin is covered, who decides? Where does it come from? Is it biblical? We are warned many times in the bible about the seductress, the prostitute, the wayward woman. Are we ever specifically warned any single one of those times about her immodesty? About her nudity? (Interestingly enough, we are never warned about the seductive man in the Bible. Why is that?) By regulating "modesty", in part based on the coverage of clothing, could we not render *any* part of our anatomy "immodest" by simply keeping it covered? Is there ever a setting by which some amount of sexual, provocative attire could actually be more "immodest" than just simple nudity? As with any of the other magnificent beauties in creation, is it not possible to *genuinely* enjoy the beauty of the human being without lust? Without sin? As with many other *choices* in life, it's a heart issue.

According to God's Word, there is a right way of thinking and behaving and we should certainly pursue that way – His Way, the Word says. In Isaiah 55:8 it says that our ways are not His ways and in 1 Corinthians 1:27 it says that God chooses what is considered foolish in the world to shame the wise. I've had many people criticize this book and say that these ideals are unobtainable in this fallen world, that while what I say is true and genuine, it's just not reasonable given the condition of our society. If we are to be in pursuit of God's plan, of perfection, of being Christ-like, of being mature, of being in this world but not of it, of being transformed by the power of Jesus Christ and the Holy Spirit, then why on earth would we not pursue the seemingly unobtainable? Is it simply because it doesn't seem possible in our feeble human capacity? God never called us to live in our power, He calls us to depend on Him, to walk with Him. If God desires for a man to be so filled with His Spirit and under His control, then the sight of an attractive nude female in his daily life should not be a significant factor in causing the man to stumble and sin no more than advertisements for delicious mouthwatering food drives a person into gluttony and obesity. I believe Paul wrestles with this very idea in Romans 7 and again in 1 Corinthians 11. His bottom line for us is that we must choose to do what is right even when faced with the temptation to do what is wrong. This will make us stronger in Christ. It's not a lack of temptations that build our faith and give us opportunity to be genuine with integrity, it's in the middle of the storms and trials and temptations to veer away from what we know to be true that we find His strength in us. If given the opportunity, are we better off to temptation-proof all of the world around us that we might not sin, or are we better off to temptation-proof our hearts and minds that we might not sin? It is not possible to remove all of the temptations from your world, but I believe through Christ and the Holy Spirit living in you that it is absolutely possible to strengthen our faith and resolve to the point where we choose righteousness no matter what temptation comes our way. In fact, the very place that a woman should be free, not only express herself, but to let down her guard with regard to her body and with regard to something like her nipples protruding through her shirt, *should* be the church. That *should* be the safe place, that *should* be the place where men *should* not lust. It *should* be the place where men see women for their beauty and respect and admire her for it no matter how she's dressed. It *should* be the very place where they don't have to spend an hour fixing themselves up in the morning before making an appearance. It *should* be the very place where they can be uninhibited, the very place where they can be *free*, the very place where they can let their guard down. What does it say about the men of God in the church if the church is the very place where women struggle the most to be on *guard* not to make men lust? Ultimately, I believe this is what Paul was saying in Romans 7 and 8 with regard to living according to the flesh verses the spirit. Yes, we are tempted, but we have the power through Jesus to make right choices, to think right thoughts, and to be victorious!

His Truth Can Replace Lies

5 Breasts

As I began to contemplate the subject matter for this book, it became obvious, really *necessary*, that I dedicate an entire chapter with focused insight into the matter of female breasts. To some of you that may have sounded a bit comical or even sarcastic, but I really intend for this to be a serious thought. If you do not know me personally (or maybe because you do!), by now you've probably labeled me to be some sort of left-wing, pseudo-Christian, pervert who is simply trying to justify a means by which I can cajole women into taking off their clothes. I know that my wife of twenty years certainly sees that as my intent and motivation with her. Given the topics of this book and the Christian culture that exists, I am sure that many of you now join her in that thinking. Straight up, that is exactly what *effect* I hope this book will have, not only on the married women, but also on the married men. However, that could not be farther from the real intent of my heart when it comes to many of these long-held beliefs and the motivation to challenge them.

At the very heart of so much of the tension with regard to nudity, provocative attire, lust, sexual desire, shame, embarrassment, awkwardness, inhibition, perversion, sin, and indoctrination, are the female breasts. The world uses a lot of slang and often makes light of this beautiful portion of the female anatomy, but *breasts are a real source of uneasiness and grief among Christian men and women when it comes to sexual purity and sin.* If you have not agreed with anything I've said to this point (Especially if you live in the United States), you cannot possibly argue with that. Our culture teaches us that breasts are inherently sexual and we have been *trained* to think of them as purely sexual, as the measure of a woman's femininity, as something that melts the minds of men, an obsession, a distraction, as an object of sexuality, passion and lust. We don't find this breast "fetish" in every culture, which means it is NOT biological – it is *learned*. In an article entitled "New Theory on Why Men Love Breasts", Natalie Wolchover and Stephanie Pappas say, "In the cultural view, men aren't so much biologically drawn to breasts as trained from an early age to find them erotic".[15] Men have allowed these ideas to really cloud their mind regarding breasts and what a healthy view of them *should* be with respect to a ladies' beauty, sexuality and person. We really battle a rushing river of propaganda that uses breasts and women to peddle everything from TV game-shows, to birth control, to food, to prescription drugs, and the list goes on and on. It's no wonder that our men and our culture are obsessed with breasts! However, it is not biblically any different (from a sin perspective) for me to have an obsession with videos games, TV, food, hunting, sports, manufactured beauty or movies and many other things. Our God is a jealous God! (Deuteronomy 4:23-24) As we see over and over and over in the old testament with the Israelites, we are quick to make idols in our life out of just about anything. The bottom line is this – even a good thing that is taken to extremes, anything excessive can become an idol that ambushes our walk with Christ and ultimately keeps us from God's will in our lives. So

---

[15] http://www.livescience.com/23500-why-men-love-breasts.html - Natalie Wolchover and Stephanie Pappas 20160317

what can we do about it? There is no magic potion that will resolve many of these well-maintained conventions and ideas, but we aren't helping matters if we remain unwilling to make some changes in our attitudes and actions – especially within the body of Christ. Neither the secular world nor the church want us to *normalize* female breasts, but if you agree that there is a problem then shouldn't we do something? Shouldn't we change something about what we've been doing? If we don't change our perspective, our culture, and what we teach our kids, then this anxiety will only intensify for future generations. Will we continue to just pile on more shame, more guilt, more misunderstanding and more frustration onto the next generation? I believe, no... I know that this is a detraction for many in their pursuit of the abundant life.

Because of this fascination and obsession with female breasts, women (especially Christian women) tend to gravitate and live in the ditch of extreme "modesty" and timidity. (Please forgive my intentional *misuse* of the word "modesty" as it has already been established that most of us probably misuse it) Most large breasted women do everything they can to disguise the breast, its curves and especially the nipple, and even some smaller breasted women do what they can to camouflage what little they have. They wear extra layers of foam-filled bras and camisoles and vests and jackets and they are critical of any woman who doesn't. It is amazing to see some of the contraptions that exist today solely in the name of breast "modesty". It is very interesting to watch those, who for whatever reason, venture out from "modesty" and wear a low-cut top or a short dress or skirt. They will then be constantly readjusting and pulling at the edge to make it go a little higher or a little lower as needed in an effort to cover just a bit more than it possibly can. They frown at the breastfeeding mom who openly feeds her baby in the middle of a restaurant or church. In fact, many don't even encourage new mothers to breastfeed because there's just too much "modesty" at stake to give a newborn what's best for it. Isn't it fitting that Satan would use the very thing that *most* resembles life, nourishment, and mothering to twist the truth and deceive God's people - the female breast. The very most important part of creation with regard to nourishing life has been turned into a tool and a perversion for Satan's use. And we allow it to continue because we're too embarrassed to do anything about it. We really cannot blame the Christian women entirely for their stance, as they have been forced into this corner by the world on one side and the church on the other. For too many years the church has preached that women should cover up and disguise their shapes and curves, when we see no justification for this from a biblical perspective. This has been passed down from generation to generation and is so ingrained in practice that even the wisest and astute women will hold fast to the notion that they must walk around in this bubble of *super* "modesty" in order to stay pure and keep their brother from sinning. The shame that women have for their breasts is so ingrained that it really is just *second nature.* (I'll reference you back to chapter one of this book and the "braless" hug of my daughter.) Nobody had to teach her that behavior, she cannot even articulate why she does this, it just came as a result of her peers, the church and the world she observed around her. What about the girl who by the age of 13 is carrying around a set of "double D's"? *What* is she to do?

Some of this problem stems from a lack of communication from parents and family, but oddly enough I think most of the resolution has to come from the same place. In fact, most of the influence for a Godly perspective in this matter will have to come from good, Godly women who will do the *right* thing even in the face of adversity from the world, and *especially* in the face of intense scrutiny from the church. I know that every family is different, but let's be honest, do you ever have frank conversations with your 10-16 year-old boys and girls about breasts, puberty, sexual feelings or nudity? I'm not talking about the "one-on-one mother-daughter let's-go-pick-out-your first bra" conversation. I mean the "open, dinner-table, everyone's-in-the-room, let's talk about female breasts tonight" conversation. Why not? Why can't we talk about our bodies? We all walk around in them, we all have very similar issues with them, and we all have very similar apprehensions about our form, as very few of us would say that ours is "perfect". I submit to you that the only reason we cannot have this discussion openly is that we've been conditioned not to, and because we are embarrassed. God created our bodies and called them good, so I doubt you will find a biblical reason to avoid such conversations. Talking to people, family or otherwise, about anything remotely sexual is very awkward for most of us. Why? Some of you may say, "well I'm too fat" or my breasts are small or my breasts are big or I have hair in weird places or my skin is too white. To all of the excuses and concerns I just say SO WHAT, we are all very different on the outside! *God has made each one of us to be uniquely wonderful creations.* The reason we cannot have these conversations is that most of us feel that our bodies are inadequate or ugly or abnormal in some way that we just want to keep to ourselves. The fake, digitally enhanced models on the magazine covers have led us to believe that there are indeed many "perfect" bodies out there among us, and they set the standard for the assessment of ourselves and others - *a standard that is not even close to genuine.* If that weren't enough, women can now get apps on their phones so that all of their selfies show a perfect complexion every time, without question and without effort. *This is not reality!* Selfie dysmorphia is fueling the fire as young girls have instantaneous access to "perfection" on the screen of their phones. Even though filtered selfies often present an unattainable look, they are blurring the lines between reality and fantasy for this segment of our society that is already largely distraught. What are we doing to our poor young girls? How could they ever grow up with a positive self-image given what they are taught is *normal*? We have refined and defined and confined beauty down to something that has to fit into this tiny, little, *impossible* box. When in reality, as many of you will attest, so much of the time beauty is strictly in the eye of the beholder anyhow. One of the problems that I see is that the beauty doesn't trust the beholder. You question whether the beholder (most of the time husbands) is telling you the truth, because you have the rest of the world screaming at you - that beauty must fit into this little box (your hair has to be died, your nails must be painted, hair has to be curly, but not too curly, or straight, or highlighted, and the list goes on and on) – whether your husbands like it or not – what everyone else says matters *more*. Is that right? Best I can tell, this goes totally against what we're taught in the Word with regard to the relationship of husband and wife. (1 Cor 7:1-16) In our society and culture, a wife's concern for what the world thinks of her matters more than that of her husband. Totally backwards.

While some of you may be thinking, "why do we even open this can of worms, what possible good can come of it?" I am not alone with my notions regarding the subject. David Hatton sheds some much needed light on the subject as he says "Christ's followers ought to *lead* the rest of the world in gratefully welcoming the sight of breasts, whenever and wherever they are displayed in *wholesome* ways. But, by redefining them in terms of body shame, the Western church laid a firm foundation for their misappropriation by the porn industry, whose particular success in America has created a pornified culture. Our nation is perversely and progressively breast-obsessed. This notorious breast-sexualization has betrayed our women and *the* Artist Who crafted their bodies. But, while claiming to honor both, many ministers and Bible teachers are guilty of deliberately participating in this betrayal."[16] There also exists a site called "007 Breasts"[17] that really provides some very candid information and explanations about the whole breast obsession. Maria Miller, the author of the site, really makes quite a few effective points with regard to the taboo, obsession and breastfeeding. The clear intent of the information provided there is to

---

[16] David Hatton, RN 2017
http://www.pastordavidrn.com/files/Breasts.html
[17] www.007b.com

sexually desensitize both men and women with regard to breasts, breastfeeding and bras, which in my opinion and hers, is exactly what needs to happen. There is another article written by Doyin Oyeniyi[18] that discusses some realizations that she had that helped her stop feeling ashamed of her breasts. These realizations were that nipples aren't disgusting or offensive, there's nothing wrong with how breasts look *naturally* (braless) and each woman *should* be the one who controls how she feels about her breasts. Sadly, most women are so indoctrinated by the world that they cannot possibly even make this distinction. They have been brainwashed from such an early age that they see bras as a natural and normal part of their body. So much of the time I find that women are their own worst source of criticism. My wife is really much more concerned with the acceptance of her appearance by the women in her life than she is with me or other men or even God. Now to some degree I certainly understand and accept that, as I am by no means a fashion guru. However, this is an area that is completely out of control and certainly one that we'll discuss a bit more later.

With regard to breasts, another specific problem area when it comes to our culture centers around the nipple and areola. Even when clothed, just the outline or protrusion of female nipples can cause anxiety, embarrassment and shame for the woman and those around her. There are a couple of reasons for this which are both still related to our current culture's obsession with the female breast and the objectification of them in advertising, media and the church. The culture and the

---

[18] Everyday Feminism

media have really served to heighten women's sensitivity to their nipples by over-sexualizing them through movies, pictures and the Internet. It is kind of interesting that we Americans, by law, do not consider the female breast to be "exposed" unless some part of the nipple is visible. This is no more evident than when there is an incident either on TV or in public and a woman's nipple is "accidentally" exposed to the world. Yet we don't think much of it when *most* of a woman's breast is exposed either by way of a low-cut top or skimpy bikini – so long as that "immoral" nipple is not visible. Most women would rather you just not know that they even have nipples, much less ever be able to see an outline or protrusion of them through their clothing. Funny that just 40 years ago there were bras on the market that had built in nipples as to give the appearance of bralessness, but with the boost of a bra. On the surface, I support much of what the "free the nipple" campaign stands for, but due to some of the motivations for the movement, it has really just served to heighten nipple shame in women – especially Christian women. Why are we so oversensitive to women's nipples when we don't even give it a second thought for a man to go completely topless? If the nipple is really the problem, then how come we don't have the same level of scrutiny with regard to men? We don't make this distinction with male and female noses, or ears, or elbows, or knees, etcetera. If I were to show you 100 pictures of nipples – careful to show *just* the nipples – of women and men, in some cases you would have a hard time picking out which were female vs. male. Now you might say, well men's nipples are not viewed as sexual and we see them all of the time - so it's no big deal. Exactly! *So why is that?* And did you know that this has not always been the case? Why don't we see men's nipples as sexual? Are they? How come the outline or protrusion of a man's nipple through a shirt is not a source of embarrassment or shame? What really is the difference? Is there ever a mention in scripture of covering of female breasts? Of hiding the outline of a nipple even through clothing? It is amazing to me that in most department stores and malls that I visit, the men manikins have obvious nipples, but most of the women manikins in the same store do not. We are being deceived.

We have fashioned this entirely through legalism and our over-sexualized culture and really the reaction that the church has had with regard to the world's exploitation of female breasts. If you are still with me (maybe not in agreement, but still reading at least) and you're irritated with what you've read so far, then I would ask you to answer the question: Why? Is it because you simply don't agree with what I have presented, even if you know there is some truth to it? Is it because you've been confronted with some unconventional truth and would rather just not face it? Is it simply because *you* think I'm wrong and this book may lead Christians astray? Maybe deep down in your heart, it could be that you agree, but what can or even should be done about this now? What's the purpose?

Isn't it amazing how some trends and fashions really develop or how we gain courage and boldness and confidence in ourselves and our beliefs when we have a group of people who stand with us! We see this so often in children, but it can certainly be observed in adults later in life as well. Women especially need other women to take up their cause when they venture out to do something against the grain of society and culture, something that will draw criticism. However, it takes a very bold, courageous woman who is very secure in her self-image and faith to step out against the grain and change that thing that has been "normal" for so long. Women are inspired by women who do things that go against the cultural norm, for that matter people are inspired by people who do things that go against the cultural norm. Now I understand that this isn't always carried out or in support of issues that are positive or even biblical. For example, this would not hold true at all for some Hollywood celebrity who may just be stepping out of the "norm" to gain some extra fame or attention in doing something outlandish. For change to really be of a good, Godly, and well-intentioned movement, it would have to start with well-respected women who could straightforwardly gain the respect and admiration of Christians, churches, and pastors. For anyone else who might try to incite change like this, it would likely end only in ridicule and embarrassment. I have witnessed this kind of change many times with my wife and other females I see in my daily life.

Maybe it appears that what I am advocating here is that good, Godly women let their guard down and migrate to what the world and the church would tell you is the "slutty" side of the road with regard to your attire. No, what I am advocating is that we begin to teach our kids that our bodies are not something to be ashamed of, and that just because the world will exploit them at every turn, does not mean that they are shameful. Not only that, but there really is no scriptural basis for us to hide every curve and protrusion behind patterns of foam, cloth and cardboard so that no one can see the shape of our body. *Women have nipples.* Did you catch that? Does it embarrass you to read that? In fact, we all have nipples. And yes, women are more attractive and beautiful because of their nipples – I imagine if you polled a group of honest women they would say the same thing of men. And yes, if the silhouette of a woman's nipples are discernable through her clothes, *I notice.* I may even smile at her and think to myself, wow, that is a beautiful woman, she has beautiful breasts, and she is confident in who she is. However, if my heart is right with God and I'm not obsessed with her, if I *refuse* to let the world distort my view, that is where it will end. I won't covet or lust after the woman by trying to seduce her or lure her into an adulterous relationship just because I notice that she's beautiful and has nipples! Though the world would teach me to think otherwise, the thought does not even cross my mind that she is in any way a slut or tramp or a vagrant of any sort. I respect her even more. She's simply beautiful, and I can simply appreciate that. So here are the concerns and questions: Either as a result of going braless or just as a result of her choice in clothing, what is "wrong" with a woman's nipples protruding through her clothing in public? Where does this shame come from? Is it from God? Is there anything "wrong" with a man noticing this and admiring the beauty and femininity of the woman? If your answer to these questions is yes, then why? Can you answer the "why" without making assumptions about all men or all women? Or is your answer "just because that's the way I've always looked at it"? Why has this become taboo? Was it a result of the world's actions or God's people?

For many of you, the answer to that last question has a lot more to do with women than it does with men. Because is it so ingrained in our society and our Christian culture, you will certainly feel "slutty" or "immodest" around your lady friends if it becomes known that you aren't wearing a bra or that the foam and padding in your bra is not thick enough to conceal your nipples. You've been trained to believe that every woman, no matter the size or shape, must wear some sort of nipple concealing apparatus to be accepted. In fact, most of the pressure on women is not from the perceptions of men, but really with the attitudes of other women. There is this socially *imposed* idea that the natural shape, dare I say God-created shape, of women's breasts is *lewd* - that every woman must *comply* with the reshaping of them into this *invented*, uniform standard or be shunned and ridiculed and slandered if they do not. This is not "modesty", the world and society has convinced you that you must do all you can to conceal the fact that you are a woman... *and you have nipples!* Embrace who you are in God's magnificent creation, *breasts and all!* Nipples and all! Women, for as much as you want men to respect you, to honor you, to not look lustfully at you, you have to be willing to bury the shame that you carry for your breasts if you expect men to view you differently. Surrender to God the shame that you carry for your breasts, it will then be the fault of men if they continue to be uneasy, shocked, and lustful with regard to them. They're not going to change their views if you don't change yours. If you do not give glory to God in your body, if you do not stand up for a wholesome perspective of breasts and nipples, if you do not engage the men who might look at you the wrong way, how will we ever change them? Why are you allowing the world to cause you anxiety and shame with regard to your body when it was created and called *good* by the ruler of the universe? What basis do you have for the shame that you feel about your breasts? If like the situation in the garden, the only answer is because the world (or as it was in the garden – Satan) has told you that your natural shape is lewd, then I would ask you – what does God think about that? What does God think about you *allowing* the world to define the perspective about the body that *He* created and called good?

6 The Contraption

By now you have certainly formed your *opinion* of me and the ideas I have presented, and you most certainly are either outraged or intrigued (or maybe you're just laughing). Please don't let this deter you from reading the rest of the book, there's still some really good stuff in the second half! If you were to sit down and talk to my wife, the one thing that she would tell you that is *absolutely* true about me is that I have done my homework. In fact, over the last several years she's probably had her doubts as to the validity and straightforwardness of my "study" and research on many of the topics presented in this book. I've read countless books, blogs and articles and listened to many sermons that touched on the topics discussed in this book. If this is true for any area at all, this is certainly the case for my exposition regarding the bra. You may be saying yeah, but you have never worn one, you have never had breasts, and therefore you have never known what it's like to go publicly with or without a bra. True, true, and true, but I have read the thoughts and ideas and frustrations of hundreds, if not thousands, of women who do and who have. I know this doesn't qualify me as an authority on bras, but it does give me some credibility to offer some perspectives from real women with breasts and nipples who wear (or at least used to wear) bras.

Let us go back to a time prior to the bra, before it was fashion, before it was "modest", before it was uplifting, before it "prevented" sagging, before it was enhancing, before it was used to hide those *"awfully scandalous"* nipples, before it was even "necessary". That there was even a time when the bra did not exist should be reason enough to at least question its declared "necessity"! Many women have been trained, really brainwashed, into believing that they must wear a bra and that it is absolutely necessary to maintain their dignity, "modesty", Christianity and pride - as well as hold their breasts up. If you are a female reading this, you probably just took *immediate* offense to that statement, and would then ask me "how could you know this?" Honestly, because I see it every day. You would too if you had grown up without this indoctrination. I see my daughter and countless other young ladies, who because of age or genetics, have hardly any breasts at all, *yet they wear bras*. I see elementary aged girls at my children's school and church who obviously have no "need" for support, *yet they are made to wear bras*. When did it become necessary for young ladies to wear bras based on their age and *not their breasts?* A better question might be, *why* did it become necessary for young ladies to wear bras based on their age and not their breasts? I am perplexed at the notion that little girls who are years from puberty are *cultured* to wear bras and *refined* to *want* to do so. We are attempting to fix the world's perverted view of breasts by doing all we can to make them non-existent. How awkward it would be for a young girl in our culture to have someone notice that she has nipples!

Most of the ladies reading this probably wear a bra and have done so since well *before* puberty - whether you "needed" to or not. However, most of you really had no idea, at the time, why you started wearing a bra, other than your mom said you should, and you thought it was the grown-up thing to do. By now I am sure you "know" why you continue to wear a bra into adulthood, but would you be honest with me if I were to ask you - why *do* you wear a bra? Most of you who have larger breasts would answer – "because I need it to support my breasts". Some of you might answer by saying that you need it to keep your breasts from moving or bouncing or jiggling! Some of you might say that "without a bra, I feel my breasts sweat when they lay against my torso". Still fewer of you would be honest enough to tell me that you wear a bra because without it, people would hardly even notice that you have breasts. The main reason for most women is simply to cover or hide your nipples, but very few would be honest enough to say so. For the vast majority of you, the latter answers are the only truthful ones, but even for the ones who honestly think they need support, you *could* be mistaken. I know that most females have *closed their minds* to the possibility that the bra is an *unnecessary* contraption in their daily public life, and I understand to some degree the pressures that drove you to this place. Very few of you will even be honest with yourself in your own mind. *It may enrage you to read the truth, much less dwell on it, or consider it.* You cannot even *consider* the possibility that you could have a more abundant life without a bra and without the shame that comes with a pair of breasts and nipples being a part of who God made you. You may not can even consider my making such a statement with regard to such a taboo and yet still claim myself to be a follower of Jesus Christ. It may really challenge everything you think you know to consider that God led me to write this book and include such an idea. Yet I believe He did. I stake my very life on it.

No matter the size of your breasts, have you ever gone completely bra-free or support free for an entire month while still going about your normal daily life? Statistically and practically, not very many modern-day women have ever done this. The bra has become an extension of your body, but certainly one that God did NOT create. *So how do you know what the outcome would be?* You simply do not. How do you know if it would be good or bad? Without testing and trying, you simply do not know. I'm not talking for an afternoon or a day or even a week, but for a good solid month to be away from the house, out in public, at church, to the doctor, to pick up the kids from school, to the grocery store, for the *whole* of a month. There are many surveys and studies and books and blogs that suggest that a bra is unhealthy in *many* ways, and not *one single bit* of information or evidence that says it helps you in *any* way whatsoever. Read that again... *what if it's true?* However, there are many doctors and studies and much research and many, many testimonies that suggest and in some cases prove that the bra plays a role in causing breast cancer, back pain, shoulder pain, breast pain, cysts, nerve damage, creases in shoulders and abdomen, breathing problems, digestion issues, poor circulation, and more. In addition, there are no studies, no research and no opinions that say that a bra is *medically* beneficial to you at all! Not one. For that matter, how many different issues are we treating and medicating that could be completely resolved by just simply removing the bra from women's lives? How many women are suffering through the horrible side effects of drugs to treat issues that *only* exist because they wear a bra? Many suspect that there are other health related problems that result from bra usage, but if *only* some of what I've listed were true, should you really have to know anything more? Why would anyone ever *choose* to wear one of these contraptions at all? Should society force you to give up your health and physical comfort just to conceal your nipples? Or is really worth the boost in self-esteem to appear to have bigger breasts than you really do? Did God create breasts knowing that they would wiggle when you walk? *IF* you believe that the God of this universe created you, did He do so *knowing* that you would *need* a bra in order to live and be healthy and pure? You already know the answer to this question.

During the 1920s, the first medical reports linking cigarette smoking to lung cancer began to appear. Most newspaper editors refused to report these findings, as they did not want to offend tobacco companies who advertised heavily in the media.[19] In fact, in the 1930's the cigarette companies hired scientists and doctors who said that there was just *barely* enough evidence to justify the "possibility" that cigarettes could be linked to cancer. As late as the 1960's, only one-third of all U.S. doctors believed that the case against cigarettes had been established with regard to their cancer-causing effects. Now, coming up on one hundred years later, we know for certain that there is a link between smoking and cancer for *most* smokers. Sydney Ross Singer and Soma Grismaijer published a book in 1995 called "Dressed to Kill"[20], which was based on a two-year study that started in 1993 and asked 4,500 women in 5 cities

---

[20] Sydney Ross Singer and Soma Grismaijer, Dressed to Kill, (Avery Publishing Group, New York, 1995).

about their bra wearing habits. While the results of this study did not link bras to being a *direct* cause of breast cancer, the bra did prove to be linked to a higher incidence of lumps and cysts in the women who wore them for more than 12 hours a day. Since then, many doctors and scientists have chimed in to support the "possibility" that bras *could* be linked to breast cancer. Mindy Tyson McHouse[21] wrote a very in-depth article that really dissects the key points of the study and the results and at the end of the article she says "I recommend you take it off". Sydney Ross Singer also wrote a paper in 2007 titled "Bras and the Breast Cancer Cover-Up"[22] where he gives several examples of how the media, industry, and the scientific research community have tried to cover-up the research while not providing *any* studies to refute the findings. Doctor Habib Sadeghi of Los Angeles who is a co-founder of "Be Hive of Healing" also wrote a recent article on the subject where at the end he says "so why not try going braless a little more often"? He then states "the power and independence you feel this time around won't be from rejecting political oppression but from taking charge of your health and *resisting the social norms* that seek to compromise it". Alyssia Michelle[23] wrote a great article on the topic where she states "it is really important to protect ourselves and take preventative action given the correlation amongst certain factors". She goes on to say that there is evidence that bra use is not the best for your

---

[21] http://www.cancerdefeated.com/newsletters/Can-a-Bra-Cause-Breast-Cancer.html

[22] Sydney Ross Singer 2007

[23] Alyssia Michelle http://healthywildandfree.com/missing-link-bra-use-breast-cancer/

health and given the connection, it is best to make the choices to take care of your health. Jessica Hope Porter, an independent blogger, wrote "What truly shocked me was learning that bra use has a greater and more direct link to breast cancer than cigarettes have to lung cancer. This is a thought that makes all those little pink ribbons seem like a *joke* on humanity. We as women are taught early that bras are a "necessity" for "modesty" and breast support. And so we wear them *dutifully* while suffering the discomfort and unknowingly damaging both our aesthetics and health."[24] What Jessica says about the little pink ribbons being a joke on humanity is exactly the reason I wrote this chapter, and exactly the reason I have been so blunt and dogmatic. My own mother, aunts, cousins, friends and other women in my life have suffered through the assault of breast cancer. It angers me to think that this bra- brainwashing is a likely link to this dreaded impairment, and nobody hardly seems to even care. *It seems that "modesty" and aesthetics are more important than life.* At this point in time there are literally hundreds of articles, research studies by doctors, and lots of discussion regarding the "possibility" of a link between bras and cancer. The bottom line is this, in similar fashion to the very few scientists and doctors who made the *early* correlation of cigarettes to cancer in the 1920's, we *now* have a small but mounting number of them *doing the same exact thing with regard to bras and breast cancer.* Knowing how this played out with regard to cigarette smoking, is it worth your health, and really, is it worth your comfort (physically), to continue to allow

---

[24]Jessica Hope Porter http://freestylehope.com/2016/06/02/why-i-believe-in-braless/ - Jessica Hope Porter 20160602

society and your peers dictate what you do with your breasts? Besides, you'll make the world a better place and you'll put a smile on somebody's face by letting them be free to jiggle! God wants us to live!

So why not rethink this convention? Do you have any idea how it would feel or how much your quality of life *could* improve with just this one simple change? In fact, if you've read this far, most women will probably be pondering the idea for the very first time ever, *if you dare*. Up to now you probably have not ever given the bra any thought at all, but rather you've just *dutifully* followed the crowd and the advice and thinking of those who went before you. You have accepted the bra to be a "necessary" contraption that all women must *endure* in order to maintain their purity, decency and morality. As already expanded upon earlier, there is no biblical basis for this at all. Really, quite the opposite. There is a right way of thinking according to God. There are ways of living that are His ways that are very different from man's ways. If this seems to be an ideal that cannot be obtained because of the world's wickedness, should we dismiss it simply because it seems too difficult and unobtainable to us? To say that women could not possibly live bra-free because of the lust of men is to say that God's way is wrong or unobtainable if indeed He desires that women be free from a bra. Just because it seems very counter to *our* way of thinking, and just because it seems unobtainable for women to live bra-free doesn't mean that it cannot be. I have read account after account after account from women whose health has been negatively affected one way or another by the bra, but you won't find one single story about any woman anywhere who has suffered any health consequences by choosing to be free from the bra. In fact, they will all testify that their daily lives have improved drastically as a result of doing away with this unnecessary burden. Ken Smith, a breast health facilitator, speaks to this whole matter much better than I can on his website that he created and manages called breastnotes.com[25]. In some correspondence that I had with Ken, he said "convincing a woman to go against her religion, her mom's advice, and "society's moral code" all at once by (gasp) removing their bra is a tall order". He says that it took him 45 years to convince his wife of this, but she is a two-time survivor of breast cancer and has now been bra-free for more than 12 years. If you're looking for a really great place to start your research about bras and breasts, or if you're just curious about what kinds of studies and research has been done already, look no further than Ken's website. This is the very best one-stop place for an abundance of honest information about breasts, bras, and truth. But Bosarge, you don't know the ramifications of women going braless in our society? You're right, I don't. But let me ask you, if it's the right thing to do and if it's healthier for the women, and if it is God's will, does it really matter what the ramifications are? Does it matter what you and I think about it? No, not one bit. There is really nothing to lose and everything to gain. Like so many of the women I have read about and hear from, you will probably be pleasantly surprised at how well the change is received, and it is very likely that you will inspire someone else to do the same. Ultimately, you could even be responsible for extending and enhancing the lives of countless women all around you. You will *feel*

---

[25] Ken L. Smith – breastnotes.com 2018

better, you will *look* better, you will save money and time, you will feel more connected to your sexuality (which will be good for your marriage), and you will be helping the next generation of women and girls. Go ahead, take it off, *throw it away*. To God be the Glory!

7 Defining Beauty

Male or female, some of us think our body is perfect, and some of us have near perfect bodies, but think they are dreadful. Some of us go to great lengths to keep ourselves looking and feeling good, and some of us seem to have never done anything at all to even try. Some of us are way too hard on ourselves, and some of us need to get busy. Many of you are never satisfied with your body and never will be, but many of you are satisfied to simply keep eating and loafing with no regard for the consequences. In living life and in reading books and blogs and such throughout the last few years, it's become plain to me that most men and women *do* care about their health and appearance. However, there are really very few who are able to do so while staying out of the ditches. The extremes are always easy to spot and ridicule and usually for good reason - it's plain to see what they need to do in order to "fit" the model a little better. I would submit to you, as I have already alluded to earlier, that most are striving to "fit" the wrong model anyhow. So you may ask, well who decides? Who sets the standards for health and beauty? Ultimately, God has already set the standard, but if you are married then you have chosen a partner and they should have a say in *your* standard. The Bible says in 1 Corinthians chapter 7 that the wife does not have authority over her own body, but the husband does. It then says likewise, the husband does not have authority over his own body, but the wife does. Even as Christians, I'm not sure we have *any* regard for this in our modern-day relationships at all. I think that this is one of those verses that we wink at and then go about our own selfish way of doing what we want to do. For if we were to abide by this scripture as husbands and wives, it would *radically* change our marriages, and probably our health.

I think this is where we as Christians tend to get lazy, and we compromise what we *know* to be the truth, as we muddle through life exerting as little effort as possible to make it through another day. Quite frankly, this is where I have the most trouble as well. On the one hand as a husband, I am to love and cherish my wife and do my best to live out 1 Corinthians chapter 13 so that I exhibit Godly, erotic love to her. On the other hand, according to Chapter 7, I am given complete authority over my wife's body. Her beauty *should* be defined exclusively by me and what I like (within reason). This is really the one area of our married lives where we are *given* permission by God to be selfish to some degree – to have things our way. Chapter 13 of 1 Corinthians says that love does no insist on its own way and it is not resentful. In some ways, chapter 7 verse 4 appears to be an exception to this verse in chapter 13, but only in the context of marriage. After all, how can we have complete authority over our spouse's body and yet not insist on our own way? I'm not sure about current times, but there was even a day when in our wedding vows we state to each other that "forsaking all others we will be faithful exclusively to the other". By no means do I have this all figured out, but given these couple of verses I can tell you that many women (and some men) are really striving to achieve the wrong standard when it comes to their bodies and their attractiveness. Many of you will simply dismiss this and say, "Well, I'm just not willing to give my spouse complete or even partial authority over my appearance". Like many other biblical directives, there is a balance that must be achieved so that we hopefully reach mutual agreement and maximum satisfaction in our married lives together. I also realize that I am a bit culturally "abnormal" in my thinking, and this is reflected in what I consider beautiful or erotic in our modern, western culture. I believe this is the beauty of a marriage and a demand of the vows taken for both the husband and the wife. Each will bring something obscure and out of the "ordinary" to the union, and each must *choose* to embrace some of these things about their mate, even if they don't feel the same way. (Hopefully we know about these things before the wedding and not after!) Notice that I didn't say that we have to embrace *all* of them, but we are certainly called to step out from what makes *us* comfortable as individuals, or from what is easy, in order to satisfy our spouse and fulfill our marriage. Sometimes this may be awkward or embarrassing for our spouse in view the watching world around us, but the genuine love we have for our spouse is the best way to overcome any ridicule. If it is for the good of the relationship, then we should strive to do everything we can, within the bounds of scripture, to please our spouse and Love them.

Most of you in the United States (men or women) would look at a woman who has allowed the *God-created* hair to grow under her arms today and say that she has poor hygiene, when in fact it really has nothing to do with hygiene. In fact, if hairy armpits were telling of a person's hygiene, then most all of the men on the planet have terrible hygiene! (I know, most of us do have poor hygiene when compared to you ladies – I agree) Too many women give "authority" over their bodies to their girlfriends or family or culture without even realizing they've done so. In my opinion and according to 1 Corinthians 7:4, that authority has then been misplaced. As was asked before, should you really allow the world around you, the culture, the media, or your friends to dictate how you dress, or whether you wear make-up, or dye your hair, or shave your legs or armpits? What if a woman's naturally hairy body is pleasing to her husband? For that matter, if it weren't for the criticism, how many women would really rather just be hairy instead of shaving? You single ladies out there, *be honest*. If you are one of many who would say – "not me, no how, no way", then I would ask you again as I did with regard to the bra, *how do you know*? Have you ever let your hair grow for even a month? Like the bra wearing, most of you ladies have been shaving since before you even *needed* to do so. You have no idea what your body feels like or looks like with hair. *If* you could somehow *separate* this idea from the apprehension due to the ridicule, how could you possibly know that you wouldn't like it? Or how do you know that it *would* drive you crazy? After all, you've *never* had hair on your legs or armpits – at least not for any length of time. If you were to ever let it stay there for a while, it might actually start to feel perfectly natural – just like it was a "normal" part of your body, just like it was *meant* to be there, *maybe even like God Himself created it.* (Oh wait, He did!)

Ruth Buezis[26] asks, "Can you believe and accept what your husband says about your beauty and your body as truth? When our husbands are peeking at us, we're supposed to be thrilled." Women have allowed the world, their peers, their family, and Hollywood to dictate

---

[26] awaken-love.net

what is acceptable both in terms of size, shape, color, skin-tone, and the *hairiness* of their bodies for far too long. Because society, culture and the fashion world have dictated what a beautiful woman *should* look like for so long, for most of you it is not even possible to know what *you truly* think is beautiful - in terms of your body or in terms of the female body in general or in terms of the male body. It's very difficult to get outside of these preconceived notions when they've been the "standard" for so long, when they've been "normal" for so long. I'll go so far as to say that most men probably have the same problem when it comes to "their" ideas of beauty. Most have never seen a girl with a naturally hairy body or no make-up — they have been taught that beauty is what culture and fashion dictate. I think it has simply been a long time in the United States since women and men were free to explore beauty for themselves, without the pressures of media, magazines and now the Internet. It is no longer something that we can seek and discover, it has become something that is purchased or applied or digitally enhanced.

What about you guys? Most of you are probably shaking your heads by now saying boy this guy is *way* off – I don't want a hairy, "manly" woman! That's gross! In a similar manner as with that ladies, I would simply ask you, *how do you know?* Have you ever *had* a hairy wife? Have you ever seen or touched or made love to your wife with her God-given body hair at its natural, *normal* length? It might would just drive you crazy – *in a good way*. I'm not talking about a little stubble from the lazy days of winter when most wives and women take week long breaks from shaving. I mean long hair that has been growing for months and is soft and natural and *normal* in so much as it can be in such a culture as ours. All of the evidence that we have would suggest that Eve and the women of her day probably had even *more* body hair than modern western women. *If* you trust and believe that God created the woman to be the *perfect* spouse and compliment for the man in *every* way, then I have to believe that most men would really *crave* the hair on a woman's body - *if ever given a real opportunity to experience it.* If they could ever find an escape from that little voice in their head that lies to them and says that women aren't supposed to have hair. God clearly meant for women to have hair on their bodies, *it's there!* If God created her to completely and *specifically* satisfy the sexual appetite of man, then why is it so hard to believe that most men would probably be the same today, if it weren't for the brainwashing of our current culture? *Are we missing out on something wonderful?* Have we allowed the world to rob us of a gift that our heavenly father created *especially* for us – specifically for us? If ever given the opportunity to know, I think that many of you would find out that it has. What other pleasures or gifts are we overlooking or sacrificing that God intended for our good? For abundant life? For an abundant marriage? We have come to associate the natural, normal body hair of females with masculinity, when this is not reality at all. Just because women shave their legs and pits (and many shave a lot more than just that!) doesn't make them any less hairy than the males. It's kind of like the transgender person having surgery to replace their outer genitalia with the opposite sexual parts, they will still be *distinctly* the gender that God made them to be. It is stamped with DNA on every single cell in their body, and there's nothing they can do about it. The removal of hair from a woman's body does not make her any *more* feminine! We have *fashioned* this idea in our minds and we have bought into it as being part of what defines a female human being, when in reality it has nothing to do with it at all. It's not genuine.

So woman of God, why do you shave your body? Really? What is the truth? Do you *even* know? Do you like to do it? For the vast majority of you, especially the single women, the truth is that you do it to fit in. You do it so that you won't stand out. You do it because you would be embarrassed not to. You do it because you have to... in your mind. There is no choice. It is an absolute of the modern western woman. You have never even questioned it. It is your duty.

Now, read Romans 12:2 - the New Living makes it plain, but any translation will say the same thing - Don't copy the behavior and customs of this world, but let God transform you into a new person by changing the way you think. Then you will learn to know God's will for you, which is good and pleasing and perfect.

All of the real reasons that you shave your body are the exact reasons that God (through Paul) says that you should NOT. Conformity with the world. God is calling you to be different - on purpose - so that you *will* stand out. The New Testament is full of scripture that pleads with us to *turn* from the ways of the world, to be different *on purpose* and for *a purpose*, that this is God's will for us. The scripture is also full of truth with regard to testing and examining our ways to be sure that they are true, that they are healthy, that they are of God, and to know why we do what we do. (Prov 1:32, 14:15, 16:4, 16:17, 2 Cor 13:5, Rom 12:2) But we don't. We are really afraid to. We don't want to deal with the consequences of the testing. *Because if we test, then we will know the truth.* Because we don't want to be different. We really want to just fit in, to just go with the flow. To just be what the world says we should be. Even if it costs us. Even if it robs us. Even if it's painful. Even if it kills us. Even if it separates us from God. This was the way of the Pharisee.

So given the stigmas, the media, the tradition and culture, you can see how difficult it *can* be to really define or determine what *genuine* beauty looks like from a pure perspective. Though I've focused a good bit on body hair as an example in this chapter, I think you can begin to see how this conversation could apply to many of our "learned" ideas about beauty – makeup, hair dye, surgery, etc. There are so many opinions and demands coming from so many directions, that even if we can determine what *genuine* beauty looks like to us, we often just keep it to ourselves for fear of rejection or embarrassment to step outside of the norm. Like I said already, how much of the abundant life are we missing out on in marriage simply because we aren't willing to step outside of our cultural boundaries and take hold of what God promised us. Husbands and wives, do not continue to allow this in your marriage, boldly step out and do the *right* thing when it comes to pleasing your spouse with your beauty and your body. Proclaim to the criticizing world that the love for your spouse is *more* important than its phony version of beauty. Be genuine!

8 Manufactured Beauty

Regardless if you agree with me on the notion of nudity and the beauty of the human body, we cannot possibly define beauty today without also discussing the idea of "manufactured" beauty. Like many controversial topics, the separation and discussion of natural versus manufactured beauty is one of those matters that can be very difficult. Consequently, there are people on both sides of the issue who will take one stance or the other and provide a myriad of reasons behind their chosen side. I simply want to motivate you to think about the side you're on, make sure you know *why* you're there, and *how* you got there. I think in a lot of ways, the beauty "industry" has done to beauty what pornography has done to sex. It has made it out to be something more than it really is, something different than it really is, much more appealing than it really is. In the end, it just leaves normal, natural, "ordinary" beauty to be unstimulating and undesirable, just like pornography leaves real people and real sex to the real man or woman. The fake has become so much the norm of our day that the real, unpainted, un-retouched, unmanufactured appearance of the female is boring. There are so many things that women do to their bodies without really knowing why, or without really understanding the consequences. I would dare say that most women and most men just go with the flow of whatever is "normal" today. At some point, there's really nothing that you can do to your body that won't gain enough popularity to be "normal" by somebody's standard. So begin to ask yourself, what is my motivation to dye my hair? Curl my hair? Straighten my hair? Wear makeup? High heels? Shave my legs and armpits? Paint my nails? Get a tattoo? Belly ring? Nose ring? I could go on and on. So much of what Jesus was trying to teach us in the New Testament dealt with our motivations and our heart. As we've already discussed, this was exactly what he was saying in Matthew 5:28 with regard to looking at a beautiful woman – it is certainly okay to look, just don't take it all the way to lust. It's also what I believe Paul was saying in 1 Timothy 2 with regard to the outward adornment of women in terms of jewelry, clothes, hair, etcetera. Just think of all the things that the world does simply to attract our attention, so as to make us envious of people who have things or achieve "beauty" that we don't have or cannot achieve. We often do more to attract attention from the world, or fit into the world, or "impress" people than we do to save them or reach them for Christ. So what's your motivation? Is it really to glorify God? Do you think He loves you more as you transform the "you" He created into something "better" every morning in terms of your "beauty"? Are *you* more concerned with your outward appearance than He is? (1 Peter 3:3) Men, are you more concerned about your wife's outward appearance than you *should* be? Have we turned this idea of beauty into a competition? Into our focus? Have we turned it into something that God never intended? An idol? I believe we have. Yet it has become so "normal" that we cannot see it. We are blind. To take a stand against it, to turn and go the other way, to choose to get out of the flow would so ostracize a person that it would devastate them. Our pastor recently preached a message out of Exodus 31 and 32 where the people had made an idol, a golden calf, and they were giving credit to this thing that they had made for their deliverance out of Egypt. They were actually discrediting God's deliverance and giving credit to a man-made idol for their freedom. So I ask you, what makes a woman beautiful? Lipstick, makeup, hair dye, high heels, bras, - are we giving credit to these man-made things for the beauty of women? Do we discredit God in some ways when we place so much value and emphasis and time on these external adornments?

The difficulty I see with manufactured beauty is with placing a boundary on its use so that it does not become a hindrance for others or an idol to the person using it. Where do you draw that line? Is makeup OK? Breast implants? Removing a couple of ribs? Dying your hair black at the age of 75? Labiaplasty? In and of itself, there is nothing biblically wrong with any of that, *or is there?* Romans 12:2 says that we are not to be conformed to this world and Galatians 5:26 says let us not become conceited provoking and envying one another. *Now I'm not saying that all you ladies should just let yourself go*, but 1 Peter 3:3-4 says that you have some control over your beauty and that it should *not* come primarily from outward adornment. Yet, if you were honest, most of it does. Look at our world today. Specifically, look at women today. It used to be that we could look at the magazine covers at the checkout line, but now-days all you have to do is be-"friends" on Facebook or "follow" a few ladies on Twitter or Instagram and you're bound to see what I mean. It's one thing to build some facades into your body by way of hair dye, breast implants or makeup, but now we can make ourselves *look* perfect with just a few swipes of our finger on a smartphone. There are people I know (yes, all women at this time) who I see in person and then I see the pictures they post online, and I just wonder about their grip on reality. Can this *possibly* be healthy for your self-worth? To see all of the comments and compliments on social media about what you *know* to be false information about yourself. When you stand in front of the mirror at night after a shower and see a completely different person on the outside, does that bother you at all? Are the husbands of these women comfortable with knowing that the perception most people have of their wife's "beauty" is fake*? Is that really beauty at all?* Where do we draw the line? Is there no end to the "perfection" that can be achieved through surgery, makeup, plastic, paint and digital image enhancement? As the extremes of yesterday become the new normal for us today, do they also become somehow more acceptable to God?

I for one have decided that the "real" is more beautiful than the "fake" because the real goes deeper into the skin and hair than the surface, and I know there are those of you out there who agree. I would rather have some unique "imperfections" in my spouse than to have manufactured beauty and "fake" "perfection". Kyle Bedford[27] is a single dad and a blogger who had this to share on the subject:

> "This whole notion of manufactured beauty disturbs me as a father and a man. Soon enough Sunshine (his daughter) will come across these types of photos and in all likelihood begin to question if she actually measures up. Does she have the 'look', the same clothes, the hair, is she too fat? Will she strive to be like 'them' in order to feel beautiful and popular. Likewise, my son

---

[27] http://chopperpapa.com/

could come to believe that a girl is only worthy of his attention if she is able to match up to the girls on billboards or the latest A&F catalogue.

One critique asked 'Can this be stopped?' I don't have that answer but what can happen is that, as men, we can stand up and influence how our girlfriends, wives, daughters, friends and family internalize these messages. We must because these 'monthly mags' are aimed squarely at the women in our lives and the target audience is getting younger by evidence of publications like Seventeen and Girls Life. But it's going to take more than just words like 'you're beautiful'. If actions do speak louder, then we need to let our behaviors speak for us. We need our deeds to send the message that the current view of beauty is distorted and it must stop."

I totally agree with Kyle on this, and I often ask myself these same questions with regard to my daughter and sons. What are we doing to the next generation?

The discussion of our bodies with regard to health as it relates to beauty or attractiveness to the opposite sex can be a tricky topic to say the least. While there's nothing wrong with pursuing athletics and naturally building your strength and endurance through rigorous training and exercise, that doesn't mean that those of us who do not choose to do so should be graded by that standard in society. However, for those of you who choose to over-eat the things that make you fat and live a sedentary lifestyle, there is good reason for your family and close friends to urge you to make some changes that will improve your long-term quality of life. I've never heard from one single person who's shed a bunch of weight who said they feel worse afterwards. Like the women who choose to be bra-free, they all feel better! Both physically and mentally. While there's good reason to influence people to take care of their bodies through proper health and nutrition, there are many ways in which we allow society to pressure us that can really be unhealthy both physically and emotionally. Again, because most of this propaganda is directed at women and young girls, most of my examples here will be on the feminine side of the sexes. Remember, I'm not picking on you females, I am sincerely trying to make the way ahead a little better, a little brighter, a little easier than it might otherwise be - and maybe even a little more genuine to the watching world.

One of the struggles I have in writing this book (as you probably have noticed) is in trying to corral the subject matter into distinct sections or chapters, and as a result I must make mention again of two already discussed topics – breasts and bras. (Yes, by now you are probably thinking – "great, two of your favorites") We have already discussed how our society and culture teaches women to do what they can to hide their nipples and breasts by whatever means necessary, especially you larger breasted or larger "nippled" women (is nippled a word?). Yet, we have super-thick foam padded bras on the market for little girls and teens that are advertised to *create* curves where none really exist. If that is not already bad enough, they advertise these contraptions with catchy slogans like "ego boost" or "the double whoa"! They are even marketing a push-up, padded bikini top for girls targeting the ages of 8-12. We are teaching our girls that they "need" to have big, noticeable breasts in order to be "normal" at a very early age. So which is it – do we teach our little girls to hide and disguise their breasts or not? From where I stand, it sure seems that we're doing both. No wonder our kids are so confused when they come into puberty in a world (both Christian and secular) that sends such mixed messages about our bodies and sexuality. *No wonder my little girl is embarrassed to hug me braless.* No wonder our young men fall into lust and attraction to the Hollywood *veneers* that fill their vision on their phones and computers and TV. We are brainwashing them to have a very skewed and very artificial idea of what a woman *should* look like – of what a *real* woman *actually* looks like. Bras skew our vision of normal by forging a false shape and lift, and we then reason that perfectly, perky breasts are the norm - all the way to age 95! (Don't believe me, just look around.) If every woman were to go braless for a day, we'd soon realize just how flawed our idea of "reality" is when it comes to the shapes, sizes and "perkiness" of women's breasts. What if men were to do this with their chests and body? What if we wore a garment or apparatus under our shirts that would allow us to look bigger, better, chiseled, and firmer than we actually are? Buff. Solid. Cut. Large! ...but not really. Picture a "normal" guy that you know who all of a sudden shows up to church with a thicker, tighter, firmer than normal chest and shoulders – overnight! *What would you think of that?* What would you think of a guy who would do that? What's the difference in this vs. the "ego boost" or "the double whoa"? What makes this acceptable for women? What have we done? Where are we going? I just ask that you think about it and ask yourself, *what does God think about all of this?* The answer is very plain – no pun intended.

Another disturbing trend that I see all around me, and especially with little girls at church, is the formation and participation in what amounts to "toddler" beauty pageants and dance teams. Now I'm not talking about a beautiful baby competition, but rather full-blown dance and/or beauty pageants to include hair, high-heels, makeup and seductive outfits. I am blown away at the age with which young married couples with little girls will allow and promote their pre-pubescent child to parade around like a young stripper complete with gobs of makeup, lipstick, glitter and paint. We are teaching our girls at a very young age that the beauty they possess in their normal, natural bodies is not *nearly* good enough for them to even leave the house in the morning. When are we going to start teaching them that they are beautiful just the way they are – no makeup, no high heels, no hair color, no enhancing bras, no shaving every crevasse of their body, etcetera? Do you ever wonder what God must think of all of this? *Do-you-ever-wonder-what-God-must-think-of-all-of-this?* - women should adorn themselves in respectable apparel, with modesty (not fancy, not flashy, not showy) and self-control, not with braided hair and gold or pearls or costly attire – 1 Timothy 2:9. Please stop and think about that question. Most older women don't even know what their true self looks like. They have been dying their hair so long that they truly have no idea what their genuine self looks like. They've *never* seen their real hair - only the color that they've put into it year after year, decade after decade. We live in a society here in the United States whereby there is more that is artificial about most women, than there is genuine – *especially on Sunday mornings.* To me, that is so sad. I think about this every Sunday morning as my wife and daughter are "getting ready" for church. Yet in some respects we love the genuine – old cars, old furniture, old barns, record albums, guns and such. As a society, we even like old scruffy men who are rugged and natural, masculine and genuine. The world has just chosen to shun women who are genuine, for the most part we would rather have them to be made-up and "better" than real - "Hollywooded".

Call it a preference if you like, but given the choice, I like the real better than I like the fake. If you read through the book of Proverbs and Psalms, I think you would have to agree that God feels the same way. In so many ways, I think cultures in other areas of the world probably get it right more often than we do here in the United States of Manufactured Beauty. Because of the poverty and desolation in most third world countries, they don't feel this need to make women any more beautiful than they are naturally – they simply don't have the means to do so. Is there really any beauty that God himself can appreciate in the temporary coverings or alterations that we make to our bodies? I'm not saying that there's never a time when a woman should make herself up to be a little more beautiful than natural, but this has become the standard by which most of them function day in and day out. Good grief, at one time my own wife thought she had to have lipstick just to go on a stinking bike ride!

As there is hardly anything left on the human body that cannot be "improved" upon with a little procedure, cosmetic surgery is a booming business today in the United States and around the world. Don't get me wrong, we need those doctors and their techniques and skills, but we need them for burns and accidents and birth defects. Instead, large numbers of women are having labiaplasty, thighlighting or buttock implants and even ribs removed in order to be "satisfied" with their appearance. Really? ...Really. How many people see your labia? So I hear most of you out there saying – these are extreme procedures performed on a very small number of extreme women per year. True, but the numbers are climbing rapidly and just because *you* think it is outrageous *doesn't mean your daughter will.* What is extreme today will be normal tomorrow. Where do we draw the line? *When will we say enough is enough?* If we don't convince the next generation that they are beautiful, that they're breasts are just the right size, that their labia aren't too big, that their waist is small enough without surgery and artificial enhancements, ...then who will? The world will *never* tell them that they are good, that they are beautiful, that their breasts, buttocks, labia and waists are the right size and shape. The world holds up its standard for "beauty" and *effortlessly* convinces girls and women that they don't measure up, that they *need* to be improved upon, that they can be better, prettier and more attractive.... *and that all of this is perfectly normal.* So what side are you on? Do you like the real or would you rather have the fake? I'll take the genuine any day.

In just barely scratching the surface of manufactured beauty, I haven't even mentioned all of the possible and probable health effects of the surgeries, the dyes, the clothes and the makeup. Look, I know that you can dig up trash on just about anything out on the old World Wide Web, but there are many legitimate issues with a lot of what you ladies do to yourselves on a daily basis. Even though we already know for certain that there are some detrimental effects on your health because of some of these practices, what concerns me more is what we don't yet know. The cosmetic and fragrance industry is largely unregulated. That means a manufacturer can put *any* substance or chemical they please into the products that you are spraying or smearing onto your bodies, then you breathe this all day long. Women (mostly) have put such a high emphasis on "beauty" and appearance and smelling good that they are often willing to overlook the adverse impacts of this pursuit on their health – to them, *it's just the cost of maintaining the façade.* While I do touch on this area in chapter 10, I could really write another whole book on the subject and still not really do it justice. Hopefully by now you have already begun to question some of your lifestyle choices, and you can do some research and study for yourself in this matter. The bottom line is this, at what point does your health and wellness become *more* important than your appearance to the *temporary* onlookers in this old world? Will you really allow what *they* think of your appearance to influence your health? Do you need the fake in order to maintain your pride and dignity, or can the genuine do a much better job? Does God want your priority to be your health or your appearance? How many people do you know right now who have cancer? How many of those cancer patients were self-inflicted?

His Truth Can Replace Lies

9 Marriage

If we as Christians understand and live according to the Bible, then sex should absolutely stay within the confines of marriage, and we should also agree that anytime we're talking about marriage – we're also talking about sex. Believe it or not, this is not a well understood and agreed upon principle within Christian circles regarding marriage. Josh McDowell said in his comments on Dr. Juli Slattery's book Rethinking Sexuality, "Without a biblical view of sexuality, we won't get anything right".[28] It is clear from Genesis and 1 Corinthians that the union of man and woman in the bonds of marriage should *always* include a sexual relationship between a husband and a wife. From my reading and experience, it seems that sexual *dysfunction* within the Christian marriage has become more of the norm than the exception with regard to expectations, fulfillment and selflessness. We have really allowed the world (TV, soap operas, pornography, movies, Facebook, etc.) to warp God's standard for marriage instead of allowing husbands and wives to set expectations within the relationship between one another. There are even therapists and doctors out there saying that the demands of a husband for a sexual relationship with his wife are grounds for abuse if the wife doesn't want sex. Often times a wife goes into a marriage with the baggage of tradition and false ideas handed down from her mother or the church or friends, or maybe even from her own bad experiences. She has nowhere to turn to for good, Godly advice, and

---

[28] Rethinking Sexuality, Dr. Juli Slattery 2018

she'll by no means trust her husband to help her work through the baggage to fully engage the marriage on a sexual level. In addition, the man usually goes into the relationship with some unrealistic expectations as well. The world is constantly bombarding him with images and ideas of what a woman is *supposed* to look like, and the pornography industry then fills in the blanks of sexuality and pleasure with all sorts of perversions and debauchery. To suppress and hide our sexual appetites can seem like the Godly thing to do in a world that constantly bombards us with sex, even though most of it being adultery one way or another. There are so many things that we "practice" as Christians that "seem" Godly, but in reality, they are just apprehensions brought on by the world and its *abuse* of God's plan for us. We have allowed the world's distortion and degradation of God's creation to pervert our understanding of His plan for sexuality and our bodies. We Christians have allowed the world's abuse and perversion of God's creation to determine how we live out our sexuality in relationships. How many times did Jesus rebuke the Pharisees when they went after the disciples or Himself for some rule they were breaking or tradition they weren't keeping? They even grumbled about Jesus and how he ate with sinners and "worked" on the Sabbath. We Christians are so uptight and uneasy about sex, sexuality, nudity and clothing (especially the Christians in these United States) that we are in many ways as guilty as those Pharisees with regard to their legalism and tradition. Matthew 23:25 says "Woe to you, scribes and Pharisees, hypocrites! For you clean the outside of the cup and the plate, but inside they are full of greed and self-indulgence" – the insides are dirty. Isn't this exactly what

Christianity has been doing with regard to sex for a long, long time now? We look all pious and "clean" on the outside with no *hint* of sexual appetite, enjoyment, or appeal. We go to great lengths so that the world will know that we are "different", that we are "pure", that we do not appreciate the open sexual deviance that flows rampant through society. We wear the right clothes, we use the right words, we men turn our heads or "bounce" our eyes from the beauty of a lady, we hide our protrusions (as best we can), we refrain from sexual jokes, we try to hide and cover the mistakes of our youth, and we barely teach our children anything about sex because we are ashamed of it. In fact, we even teach that shame *purposefully* to some degree. But on the inside of "us", inside our marriages, inside our families and inside our churches, *sexuality is a very different story*. In fact, from my personal experience and research, it can be ugly... quite ugly. On the inside, our sexuality is quite a mess, and in fact is absolutely upside down from how God planned it to be. It is clear in 1 Corinthians 7 that God's intention for sex was that it was supposed to be at the very *heart* of our marriages. Paul says here that we should be apart (sexually) for only a *limited* amount of time or else we'll be tempted. Sex inside of many, if not most, Christian marriages has become just about the exact opposite of what Paul describes. I'm not saying that all Christian marriages are that way, but I would venture to say that the insides of our cups and plates are *pretty* dirty when it comes to our married sexual relationships.

Scripture makes it quite clear that we are not to just do whatever we please and expect to be rewarded in spite of it. There are rules and laws with regard to our sexuality and how we are to behave with one another and treat one another. I'm not advocating that we abandon all Biblical logic and just do whatever makes us feel good at the time. But I am saying that it's time that we "Christians" stopped being ashamed of our sexuality within the confines of marriage, between one woman and one man. Wives, take down those walls of apprehension and shame and enjoy this beautiful gift that *God has created* for you. Of all creatures, you are the most beautiful and you have within you the ability to generate and enjoy pleasure for both yourself and your husband. Did you know that unlike the man, the woman has a sensory receptor whose *sole function* is to give her pleasure? Every other part of your body and every part of a man's body has a purpose for something other than just sexual pleasure, but your clitoris was created by God and its *sole function* is for *your* pleasure! Why do you put so much time and energy into suppressing the *very* thing that God gave you *exclusively* to bring you pleasure?

In the pre and post-sin Old Testament, as well as the New Testament, we only find one prohibition with regard to married sex – set aside time from each other for prayer. Obviously, there are many other important things in our lives that *must* not be neglected as well, but biblically, prayer is the *only* one that is specifically mentioned. However, if we are to live up to all of the other Biblical mandates on our lives as Christians, then we must also devote time to other things as well. My point is not that we should focus our entire waking lives on sex (outside of a little prayer time), but rather that we should not *limit* ourselves and allow other things to rob us of intimate time spent with our spouse. At the same time, we should not limit ourselves from any activity that is mutually satisfying to each partner just because *we* think that it is depraved, sinful or naughty. There might be an activity that is silly or even trivial to you, yet is incredibly satisfying to your spouse. It's important that we make this distinction, many of you are opposed to some sexual "acts" simply because you view them as naughty, not because you don't enjoy them. You've been programmed to associate them with the world, with sin or with ungodliness through pornography and perversion. One Christian blogger, Melanie Lloyd, put it like this –

> "...if we just oblige when our spouse desires to connect with us, then we will get bored. When we are just racing to the finish line to get it done, we are missing out on what God intends to be a gift and a blessing to us. Or if we are just following a routine – touch here, rub twice there and boom – we simply lose interest. Sex is about relationship, it's not a separate part of our life or a to-do list item."[29]

We cannot let our minds and our man-made inhibitions rob us of the fulfilling sexual relationship that God obviously wants us to have in a marriage. Because you have been taught for so long that your body and certain sexual acts are shameful, this problem is far more prevalent with the ladies than it is with the men. As I stated earlier, just because the world has abused and distorted God's creation doesn't mean that *we* should

---

[29] Awaken-love.net – Melanie Lloyd 2016

view it any differently, *He certainly doesn't*. Whatever He said is "good" – is still good! - It didn't change just because the world abused it! Sheila Gregoire[30] says, "I have tried so hard on this blog to teach women to get over sexual lies they've believed and know what it is to experience spiritual intimacy when they make love. I will continue to encourage frequent, fun, and interesting sex, including learning to be more adventurous in bed, because being vulnerable and a little out of control is part of 'hot and holy' sex! I will try to point women towards a fulfilling and intimate sex life, because God created us for something amazing, and we don't want to miss out! We were made for intimacy." Exactly! She went on to say in this particular entry that many women have issues with sex because of the way the church talks about it. I wonder how many couples are indeed missing out on an abundant sexual life, *and they don't even know it*?

> "If we, with our spouse, are moving our marriage toward that perfect garden and the tree of life within it, then we can safely express our joy, cry tears of worship or tears of pain, deeply grieve and be comforted, experience unrestricted passion and pleasure, and freely express our desires. We are designed to be free!
>
> When we instead 'eat' of the tree of the knowledge of good and evil, we live in fear of judgment and cannot walk in the freedom of being fully known. We cannot express all of ourselves with the abundant freedom that God

---

[30] Tolovehonorandvacuum.com – Sheila Gregoire 2016

intends within marriage. *Be certain of this, we are not designed to hide.*

God desires us to echo the Garden of Eden in our marriages. We can do that by being life givers that don't hide from our spouse or from God."[31]

Our appetites for simple wholesome pleasures come with a vulnerability to overindulge, which morphs into sin and debauchery. The bible warns us about many of these like over eating – though it's certainly no sin to eat, over drinking – though it's only a sin to drink to point of being drunk (Proverbs 23:20-21), over sleeping - though it's a necessary part of life and certainly no sin to sleep (being lazy – Proverbs 20:13), over working – though God has built our very existence a necessity to work and work we must (Proverbs 23:4), and many others. Yet with regard to our marriage and our spouse, the one thing that the bible *implies* that we *should* overdo, that *should* be in excess, that we *should* enjoy and *pursue* - is sexual fulfillment with our spouse. There are no limitations placed on our sexual relationship with our spouse, yet it has become the one thing that is most often neglected in a "Christian" marriage. There's not one verse of scripture that ever says *tone it down*. In fact, the Bible says in Song of Solomon that we should be intoxicated (drunk) in sexual love for our spouse (Song of Solomon 5:1) In 1 Corinthians 7:5 it says that we should only

---

[31] Melanie @ awaken-love.net

separate for an agreed upon, temporary time for prayer, but otherwise we should be meeting the sexual needs of one another without question, *whenever* desired.

> "If you are not being sensual in your marriage, if you are not trying to be an amazing lover to your spouse, then you are in fact violating God's commandments regarding sex, and thus are committing sexual immorality. After all, sexual immorality is going against God's plan for sex. You can't argue that sex outside of marriage is a sin without standing on the same ground and saying that sex inside of marriage, then, should be not only existent, but awesome." – Jay Dee[32]

Do you remember as a child being anxious or nervous about trying something new or different (like jumping into a swimming pool or going down a tall playground slide or stepping onto your first roller coaster), but then once you frightfully made it through that first time, you just wanted to go back and do it again and again and again? How much are we missing out on in our marriages just because we are not willing to try something new? To get that first fearful run behind us? Archibald D. Hart, a PH.D. and professor of Psychology, when talking about sex says "I believe it is that the beautiful gift God has given us has become distorted, and men in particular, have lost their way! What was intended by God to be a joyous, transcendent experience that unites a man and a woman, has become

---

[32] Jay Dee – uncoveringintimacy.com 3/20/2015

a bewildering, bothersome, and, for most, baffling challenge."[33]

We have to get back to the basics and that means that we Christians must release ourselves from the ideas of the world and return to the Bible for our standard of living – especially living the married life. Without getting into the details of the book of Song of Solomon, let's just take a look at the big picture and think about how God intended to use this book in our lives. As mentioned back in chapter 2, this book of the Bible often gets labeled as taboo or distasteful, especially by the most pious of Christ followers. Yet it *should* be considered as infallible, important and *pure* as any other book of the bible. What would God say about that? Do you think He would shun this portion of His Word as many professing Christians do, or do you think He would say that this book is possibly one of the most relevant portions of scripture dealing with the marriage relationship for our day? Think about it. As mentioned, this isn't a study of the Song of Solomon, but rather a wide angle look at the book overall to realize the purpose and apply it to our lives.

The lovers in the scripture go through a number of exchanges back and forth as they describe each other's bodies and the pleasures they desire to give and to receive from the other. In fact, the entire book really describes the desperation and passion that they feel for one another in intimate detail, and without reservation or inhibition regarding the world around them. How many of us do this with our spouse today or dare to journal about it? Most of us are probably embarrassed

---

[33] Archibald D. Hart, PH.D. – ministrymagazine.org 2002

or scared to do so for fear of rejection or ridicule. The scenes of Solomon didn't play out in a bedroom, at night, under the covers, behind closed doors and in deep secrecy, but rather the lovers speak of being outside in the orchard or near the grape vines. I dare say that our culture, our society and even our very laws would not allow this scene to play out in the modern world, but that doesn't change the fact that it did then, and it really should now. If you just read that last sentence and thought to yourself "well that's just awful, how could you say that – how could two people do that?", then you need to ask yourself why do I feel that way? Have you let the world's abuse of sex, the human body and God's plan for marriage separate you from the passion and inhibition you should clearly have for your spouse? Some may read through the book (Song of Solomon) and say well perhaps this was just one *very* special occasion that happened one time and was never repeated again with the same intensity. Really..., go read through the eight chapters again. Look at the detail in the descriptions, look at the metaphors and comparisons made and at the passion and love described and tell me that this couple only behaved this way this *one* time, and that was it. I don't think so. *This was their life.* This was every waking moment they could find outside of work, prayer and sleeping. I think this was their way of life and I think the sole purpose of the book is to provide a vivid description of what God intends for marriage. I think if Adam and Eve had described their relationship prior to the fall, it would have looked very similar. This couple had a deep, passionate, sexual love for each other and they didn't care who knew and they certainly did not have any inhibitions between them.

They were truly, one flesh. Nowhere in scripture are we ever instructed (as married couples) to tone it down, to inhibit our love or desire, to be careful with our public displays of affection or to keep our sexual affections hidden. Again, I'm not saying that we should start putting our passionate love-making on display in public places, but the world's abuse of sex has made us very apprehensive about our public displays of affection with our spouse. And though this is *exactly* what the secular world *needs* to see in our "Christian" marriages, it is *exactly* what's missing. My wife is ashamed to kiss me in public, certainly if it is a passionate long kiss. I would venture to say that most wives probably feel this way if mine does. Think about this for a minute. The last and really the only time we ever encourage and applaud and praise a married couple for passionately kissing in public is on their wedding day. Beyond that, it is most always frowned upon – especially by the church and especially at church. You may find yourself being escorted out of the church if you were to passionately kiss your wife inside in the presence of others – especially if you made a habit out of it. What is wrong with us? No wonder the divorce rate is higher in the church than outside. No wonder sex is the number one reason for divorce, period. We don't encourage the one thing that God said we should delight in. In fact, we almost seem to discourage any passion in marriage at all. That's sad.

Once upon a time, while waiting on my son to pump gas at a station, I opened the front door to the truck and start kissing my wife while the driver's door was left open on the other side. Almost immediately she tells me to stop because she's worried about the kids in the next car over seeing us kiss - I stop and say *"that's what's wrong"*. She says "I know, I know. That's what's wrong with me." I said to her "that's not what I said. This is what's wrong in the world." The last place we celebrate a married couple kissing each other is at their wedding. After that it's inappropriate to see them kissing in public. Instead of shaming this in a public setting we should be celebrating it.

We are told in scripture that our marriages are a picture of Christ and His church and He says that He might present the church to himself in splendor, without spot or wrinkle or any such thing, that she might be holy and without blemish. Many times, we (as married couples) will often say or refer to our sexual relationship as "naughty" or "bad", and I even read and hear this from other people in somewhat of a joking manner. What a huge fallacy on our part as followers of Christ, as we are unintentionally comparing the sin and perversion of this world to the very bride of Christ. If you think that passionate, intimate sexual behavior with your spouse is in any way bad or immoral, then you are also implying that Christ's relationship with His Church is the same. We are basically saying that we are participating in the sexual sin and debauchery of this world when we are passionate with our spouses in marriage. Yet Jesus says that the bride within marriage is without spot or wrinkle and without blemish. What does God think of us when we call the love and passion that *should* exist in our marriages - naughty? *He made us to be passionate for our spouses!* Again, there is but one prohibition in all of scripture for the married couple regarding their passionate sexual love for one another. ONE! What God has given to us in marriage is GOOD! It is glorious! It is without spot or wrinkle and holy and without blemish.

Stop calling it naughty and bad! Start talking about how *good* it is! To the extent that we refuse to talk about tough sexual issues, we allow culture to define God's character and truth on sexuality. Dr. Juli Slattery who I mentioned earlier has written an excellent book entitled Rethinking Sexuality. In it she says,

> "Throughout your lifetime, you have absorbed millions of messages teaching you the cultural narrative of sexuality. You have been encouraged over and over again to think about sexuality from the world's perspective."

The world, and now-days even some Christians, look at marriage, and specifically Christian marriages, and for the most part I think they say – "why bother". What a sad testament to what scripture presents as a picture of Christ and His Church.

As with many topics in this book, please don't let this just be one of those moments where you get offended or where you feel guilty and shrug your shoulders and go on with the same. Old. Dead. way. Dig into the Word, do some research, stop right now and pray and ask God to show you what you can do – what you *should* do – in order to carry out His will in your life with regard to your marriage and your spouse. THEN DO IT! CHANGE! Do NOT worry about what people think! Make a difference in the life of your spouse, in the lives of your children, and in the lives of the on looking world. Your spouse may look at you funny or they may even question your motives, but don't let the awkwardness of the subject or situation deter you from all that God has for you in terms of your marriage and your life. For married folks, if there's one area in particular that God definitely wants you to live the abundant life, it is *certainly* within your marriage. But don't let the world cloud His plan for your physical relationship, be *genuinely* enthusiastic and excited about sex!

10 Health

Though it may not make the headlines very often, healthcare is one of the most controversial, yet important, topics of our day, as there is no one among us who really enjoys pain and suffering. Although I will just barely scratch the surface with regard to a few areas that have directly affected me or my family, perhaps this will give you a new fervor to research and explore and question the food you eat, the substances you use on your body, and how and why you do the things you do. If you haven't already, I believe that you will lose some trust that has been established in big healthcare organizations, your doctors, and maybe even in close friends and relatives. At the same time, I believe you will gain insight into a new and better way of living that will help you feel better, visit the doctor less, and ultimately live longer. It wasn't me who brought to light most of the ideas and insight that I am about to share with you, but I sought books and the research of other people and simply applied what they had already figured out. Some of the ideas here will go against the grain of BIG medicine and government, and because of this you will be inclined to doubt the validity of the research. After all, who doesn't trust their doctor, or the Center for Disease Control and Prevention, or the American Cancer Society? Just remember, as bad as it sounds, big medicine and the big cancer are BIG business. Wealth, power and greed can make people do some horrific things at the expense of your health and well-being. I've already touched on this back in chapter six with regard to the bra and the cancer link cover-up that exists here in the

United States. There are some other "cover-ups" that exist with regard to your health, and we're going to explore just a few of them.

It seems that almost every day I hear about someone else who has been diagnosed with cancer of one form or another. As with the cigarettes from our discussion in chapter six, doctors have been able to pin-point some of the causes of cancer, or at least some of the links that are cause for concern. However, through research and study there are links and suggestions that have not been widely accepted, but that could be cause for concern with regard to some cancers. Much like the example of cigarettes, the links may be slow to get traction, even though many will likely prove to be accurate. One such link has to do with deodorant, armpits, shaving, aluminum, and breast cancer. While there have been no direct studies or links with regard to the aluminum in deodorant and cancer, there have been some findings that show a correlation between the two. Also, there have been some associations with regard to shaving the armpit area as the process *always* causes some minor nicks and cuts in the skin even if not visible. The process of shaving makes way for some harmful deodorant ingredients to get directly into the bloodstream and lymphatic system. As these nodes of the lymphatic system are responsible for 75% of the lymphatic drainage from the breasts, this kind of information should trigger you to stop and think about some of the things you practice in the name of "good hygiene" or "beauty". Could these practices actually be doing you serious harm, while at the same time doing you no real good? Did you know that many women (and perhaps even some men) do not even need deodorant?

Either by way of genetics or their unique physical makeup, many women who regularly use deodorant are doing so unnecessarily. Again, this is one of those things that is assumed and taught just because it is the "normal" thing to do, but it may not be necessary. To her surprise, my wife stopped wearing deodorant a long time ago, and with very little exception, no one would ever know it. Understandably, she was very self-conscious about this and quite often would ask me to smell her armpits during the times when she thought she might have an odor. To her surprise and disagreement some of the time, I don't think she's ever had a bad odor. (But I may be a bit biased) Do you know what would happen or how your body would respond if you were to give up deodorant for a day or a week? You might be surprised. Many women who have also allowed their armpit hair to grow say that the hair actually wicks perspiration away from their under arm and keeps them from smelling. SARCASM ALERT! - Imagine that, a purpose for something that God created. What do you have to lose by giving it a try? What if by simply doing away with bras and shaving we could eradicate breast cancer? What if?... Would you just rather have cancer instead of going against the grain? Against the culture? *How insane is that?* Will you choose to do anything about it? Will you change or will you just make a good showing of the pink ribbons again in October and just hope that they're never on display for you? Every time you see those ribbons from now on, think about the lives and health of those people for whom you are an influence. Could a radical change in your lifestyle actually help someone else? Absolutely. This is why the pink ribbons drive me crazy.

Given that a large portion of this book deals with our skin in one way or another, it only makes sense that I give considerable attention to the issue of skin cancer. For those of us who believe that God created us (as I described in chapter one), let us consider that He also created the earth and the sun and called them good. I am an engineer and very analytical, which sometimes gets me in trouble with folks who aren't. Why would a good God create a good planet and a good sun and then put his good people on the planet only to have the sun give the people cancer? Now I know that we live in a fallen world and pestilence and disease are just a part of the sin problem, but even so, why would the sun cause cancer in humans? And why would the incidence of skin cancer be trending worse over the last 50 or so years? How did humans survive out in the sun without sunscreen a hundreds of years ago? There are people living in many tropical climates on earth who are exposed to the sun many more hours a day and yet there is a lower incidence of cancer, even though these people groups wear little to no clothing. Marco Torres[34] wrote a very in-depth article on this very topic where he dispels the myth of the sun causing cancer. In fact, he makes a case by which we may be *increasing* our risk of cancer by not getting *enough* sun on our skin – especially here in the United States. Even worse, most of the popular sun screen products on the market today are riddled with chemical ingredients that are either suspect or proven to *raise* your risk for cancer. So we buy a product marketed

---

[34] "It's Time To Stop Perpetuating The Myth That Sunlight Causes Cancer" - http://preventdisease.com/news/15/112015_Its-Time-Stop-Perpetuating-The-Myth-That-Sunlight-Causes-Cancer.shtml

to protect us from the sun, but instead is a catalyst for cancer. Most of the time we'd be better off to just get burnt. Nice.

From a purely logical perspective, it makes sense that we western humans spend way more time indoors and out of the sun than we used to, and this could be one reason for the uptick in skin cancer. In looking at the skin cancer and non-specific cancer demographics of the world, it is interesting to note that the countries closer to the equator have a lower incidence of skin cancer. In fact, most of the underdeveloped countries have a lower incidence of cancer in general, but especially the ones in the warmest and sunniest climates. Looking at graphs produced by the CDC, the incidence of skin cancer has risen among white and fair skinned people in the U.S. staring about 1975, but the rate really increased dramatically from 1990 to present. The data also shows an increase of skin cancer back to the early 1900s when sunscreens first started being used to block UV exposure. Just think about it for a minute, has the sun suddenly (in the last 100 years or so) started to give us cancer when we humans have been on the earth for thousands of years? It is very likely that something else we are doing, or eating, or using on our skin is likely the source of grief when it comes to sun exposure and skin cancer.

Consider this, not only are the skin cancer rates lower for most of those undeveloped countries, but the availability and use of soap and shampoo is almost non-existent there as well. What does one have to do with the other? The answer actually makes perfect sense, but the methods are going to be a shock to the culture of Americans. It has already been established that vitamin

D is created naturally by the sun and cholesterol through synthesis as UV light hits our skin. I'm not going to get into the details in this book, but Dr. Joseph Mercola published an article where he explains in detail what I am about to summarize. You can view this entire article on his website which is in the footnote[35]. The problems we have with the sun – skin cancer, moles, freckles, etcetera – are mostly due to the sanitization of our skin on a daily basis. Yes, believe it or not, your daily, soapy shower could be the cause for much of the skin cancer and other skin related problems we see ramping up today. Our skin produces a substance called sebum – it's that natural oily substance that you feel on your skin or in your hair if you go without bathing (really just without soap) for a few days or so. It turns out that this substance is not only responsible for producing the much-needed vitamin D that your body uses to fight off disease, but it is beneficial to you in a variety of other ways as well. It acts as a natural sunscreen of sorts, so that skin exposed to the sun does not burn as quickly when there is a good natural layer of sebum on it. The glands that secrete the sebum are actually part of the immune system and thus the sebum also acts as a barrier to germs, bacteria, viruses, and other potential contaminants that might otherwise penetrate the skin. These same glands also produce vitamin E on the facial skin which, as you ladies know, is key to fighting aging skin. There's so much more that this incredible layer of oil does for us on a daily

---

[35] Dr. Joseph Mercola – 2009 - http://articles.mercola.com/sites/articles/archive/2009/05/12/shocking-update-sunshine-can-actually-decrease-your-vitamin-d-levels.aspx

basis, but it's obviously very important with regard to the battle against skin cancer.

Our body's ability to produce a substance like sebum with all of these wonderful benefits is the good news, but in our attempt to improve upon something that God had already perfected, we humans have failed ...again. Go figure. In our quest for ultimate *cleanliness*, we have developed hundreds if not thousands of soaps, shampoos and detergents that most of us use on a daily basis (if not more often) to "clean" our bodies. Unfortunately, in the process of bathing, most all of these products also strip our skin of this naturally occurring wonder-oil called sebum. They leave our skin bare (pardon the pun after reading earlier chapters) and dry and exposed to the sun, bacteria and disease. There is an obvious need for us to bathe, so what is the answer to this dilemma? Once again, our great Creator, in what I referred to earlier as His "intuition", has already provided the solution for the problem even before he put man and woman on the planet – simply water. That's right, the world has taught you that you need all of these chemicals and soaps and shampoos and perfumes so that you can feel and smell *better* than clean, when in reality these things are not genuine. A bath or a shower of plain water will rinse the day's dirt and smells right off of your skin and no one will be the wiser. I began this regiment myself and it went on for almost 2 weeks before I *told* my wife what I was doing. She was none the wiser by way of noticing any difference in my smell or appearance – and she sleeps naked right next to me every night. In a solid month of this practice, no one in my daily life has a clue that I've changed anything. Do we *need* to use all of these soaps and shampoos in order to clean our bodies? Absolutely not. In fact, I don't imagine that Adam and Eve had anything more than river water to cleanse themselves as needed. Once again, we have positive proof that something we all have just *taken for granted* as a *necessary* part of living, is actually degrading our life.

Now let's turn our attention back to the breast and specifically the high incidence of breast cancer that we've already touched on in chapter six with regard to bra usage. If you had a hard time considering that your bra may be giving you cancer and making your breasts sag (not to mention *detracting* from your natural God-created shape and beauty), then you're not going to like what I'm about to say any better. That doesn't make it any less genuine. Every year in October we see the pink ribbons go up and out and all sorts of walks and runs and charity fund raising events are hosted in the name of deceased loved ones for breast cancer prevention and detection. Much of this funding is used to provide a means for those who cannot otherwise afford it, to see a doctor and have a "routine" mammogram. It all *sounds* really good and many people sacrifice their time and money and lives to be able to honor their mom or sister or aunt or grandmother who passed on because of breast cancer. The term "awareness" is used on bumper stickers and magnets, billboards and t-shirts and e-mail and news to the point where there's really no way anyone could not be *aware*. So, in goes the next unsuspecting lady to have hear breasts pressed and flattened to the point of metastasis almost 80% of the time if she already had cancer and didn't know it. A large study in Canada found that women who had "routine" mammograms before the age of 50 were 36% *more* likely to die of breast cancer than those who did not. You read that right, MORE likely. In fact, many studies show NO increased survival rate from routine mammogram screening *at all* given the high percentage of false positive findings. "Last year, results from a 25-year follow-up of two landmark studies tracking about 90,000 women concluded that mammography did NOT reduce breast cancer deaths at all."[36] In findings presented in 1995 UK journal called The Lancet, Researchers wrote that "the benefit (of mammograms) is marginal, the harm caused is *substantial*, and the costs incurred are enormous"[37] In an article from the New England Journal of Medicine from November of 2012, it was stated that "our study raises serious questions about the *value* of screening mammography".[38] "Remember, 10 times as many women are harmed in some way compared to those whose lives are spared by annual mammograms."[39]I could keep quoting doctor after doctor and study after study, yet millions of women will still to go their doctor this year for their *yearly* mammogram. Why? Why? Why? The doctors, big cancer, big medicine and big government don't *want* you to know this. Do your homework and ask your

---

[36] Christie Aschwanden –
http://www.motherjones.com/politics/2015/10/faulty-research-behind-mammograms-breast-cancer
[37] Ethan A. Huff -
http://www.naturalnews.com/053935_mammography_breast_cancer_false_diagnosis.html
[38] New England Journal of Medicine Nov 2012
[39]Dr. Christiane Northrup 2016
http://www.groovybooby.com/single-post/2016/07/19/Mammography-Can-Turn-Healthy-Women-into-Cancer-Patients

gynecologist some hard questions next time you go in to see him or her.

Though I've already touched on it in several places, I must bring this problem back to the surface one more time – complacency. The Bible says in Proverbs 1:32 – "For the waywardness of the simple will kill them, and the complacency of fools will destroy them". It has become hard for my human self to feel sympathy for a woman's struggle against breast cancer when *most* seem very complacent to do anything or show any interest in fighting it themselves. If I were able to give you bonafide proof that some of the lifestyle choices you make do indeed cause breast cancer, many of you would NOT choose to change anyhow. I've already proven this to be true over and over in my interactions with women in my own life. In fact, I used the mammography statistics just mentioned above in a life group lesson that I did several months back, *and there was no reaction at all.* No questions, no gasps, no concern, no interest. I was blown away by this. Did all of the ladies in the room already have this information? I doubt it very seriously. It is amazing to me that we have so much good information at our fingertips, and yet we choose to just go with the flow, life as we've always done it, no *room* for change, and no *interest* in making it better – even if it could cost us our life, much less if it will cost us the *abundant* life.

On a brighter note with regard to breast cancer screening, thermography is starting to emerge as a much better alternative to mammography. Marnie Clark[40] states in an article from June of 2016 that

---

[40]Marnie Clark -http://marnieclark.com/category/breast-cancer-screening-2/mammogram-breast-cancer-screening-2/

"thermography is an alternative method of screening for breast cancer that is completely safe, non-invasive, does not subject the breast to harmful radiation and doesn't hurt at all!" The "good news" story with many of these debates is that there is always a good alternative to what we've be told or taught is our only or best solution. That's really the whole message of this book. Challenge what you've been taught! Know *why* you do the things you do. Don't let the world or your parents or your peers or your doctor and in some cases even the church dictate what is best for you or right in God's eyes. There are many tools at your disposal and God's Word is packed with promises and instruction for our daily lives.

I would leave you with one last thought that certainly correlates directly to our health, but can also encompass much more when it comes to God's creation and our bodies. Proverbs 16:4 says that God made everything for its purpose. I take that to mean that everything God created certainly has an intended purpose whether we see that or not, whether we understand it or not, and whether we like it or not. Man has gotten so busy with trying to alter God's purpose in such a wide variety of ways that often times we miss his abundant life plan for us. There are numerous examples out there and a few that I have already mentioned, but really the purpose for this comment is to have you look for His purpose in everyday life. Stop and consider some of the ways that man has stripped the purpose of God from his (man's) existence. This could be anything from the sebum on our skin to the very sex and sexual organs that He created for each of us to be. We're in this constant struggle to change ourselves and our world, to "improve" our bodies and our environment, to make it somehow better than He created it to be. In many ways, destroying the very purpose for which He created, and in some ways even detracting from the abundant life that He promised. So are the self-imposed "improvements" or "enhancements" in your life today really serving to bring abundance to your life? Are they genuine?

We tamper with God's order at our own peril.

11 Dabarim

The word Love appears over 500 times in the ESV[41] translation of the bible. The word Love and the actions required for *genuine* Love as shown in the Bible almost *always* refer to either people or God. When Jesus was asked "what is the greatest commandment", his answer in Matthew 22 was to Love your God with all your heart, soul and mind. He then said the second greatest was to Love your neighbor as yourself. He said all of the law and prophets were dependent on these two commands. To practice these two commands requires a selflessness that most of us do not possess in our modern age of materialism and "selfies". To practice these commands requires a conscious effort and dedication on a daily, if not hourly basis. To practice the first one with all of your heart, soul and mind will require a lifestyle whereby we walk with God daily and pray to Him constantly as we study His Word. We must choose to allow God to fill us with His spirit on a daily basis if we are to have any success at all. Few of us are able to do this, even fewer are able to do it well and do it with consistency.

Oddly enough, I believe that part of the problem with regard to sexuality and relationships is the simple abuse of the word "love" and the actions that the Bible speaks of in 1 Corinthians 13. We have so cheapened the word, and thus the actions, that it really has lost its meaning and effect in our lives on a daily basis. I'm going to pick on some of you, or maybe most of you, for just a minute. How many times a day do you use the word

---

[41] English Standard Version ©

Love? How many of those times are you referring to a person or God? It is very interesting just how freely and flippantly the word love is used in our world today. We "love" everything. We love cheeseburgers, we love pizza, we love coffee, we love phones, we love staying up late, we love movies, we love the beach, we love music, we love clothes, we love cars, we love vacations, we love hunting, we love sports, we love pictures, we love a cool breeze, we love cats or dogs, we love ideas, etcetera, etcetera. I could go on for pages and pages and pages about all of the things we "love". Just like it takes a conscious effort to follow those two great commands that Jesus gave us, it certainly also takes an effort to use words appropriately, dare I say, even biblically. The Word says in Matthew 12 verses 36-37 that we will be held accountable for every careless word we utter. I don't know about you, but that *genuinely* concerns me. The Bible speaks over and over about our speech and how we should be quick to listen and slow to speak. In Ephesians 4:29 it says that we are to let no corrupting talk come out of our mouths, but only what is good. I think we have allowed the word Love to become corrupt, and thus it has corrupted our society and our relationships. Now some of you are shaking your head and thinking, Bosarge you are just being too picky, too legalistic, to critical, and too old fashioned. Am I? The Word says in 1 John 2:15 - Do not love the world or the things in the world. If anyone loves the world, the love of the Father is not in him – yet as I just mentioned, we speak everyday about loving the *things* in this world. In fact, we do it all the time. C. S. Lewis, in his book Mere Christianity, says that we have done nearly the same thing with the word "Christian" in that it has become a term that simply describes a good person and not necessarily a follower of Christ. I challenge you to remove the word Love from your vocabulary *except* when used sincerely to address people or God. See how it changes the word for you. See how it changes the *world* for you. See how it changes your actions and how you see those around you.

Words matter. In 1 Timothy 1:15, Paul says that Jesus came into the world to save sinners, of whom I am the chief. Many times, I have felt this way with regard to my words and the harm they have done to others. Of all the warnings given in the Word of God, there is probably more scripture dealing with your words, your tongue, your talk and your speech than any other single subject in the whole Bible. Yet many of us, dare I say most of us, struggle with this on a daily, hourly or minute by minute basis as we abuse others or God with a lack of discernment in our talk. Proverbs 21:23 says "Whoever keeps his mouth and his tongue keeps himself out of trouble." Proverbs 13:3 says "Whoever guards his mouth preserves his life; he who opens wide his lips comes to ruin." Why is it so hard for us to follow these Godly ideals when it comes to our talk? I believe it is because we are all very selfish, and when we go against His Word with our speech we are almost always doing so with a selfish intent. I believe that if we could better control and use our words, then we could better live good and Godly lives by helping our neighbor, fulfilling our mates, and spreading the Gospel – genuinely.

In a world more connected in more ways than ever before in the history of man, with more information available with but a voice command, a finger tap on our phone, or a few keystrokes, and with a generation that is more hungry and ready for truth than ever before, our communication with one another is probably more pathetic than it has ever been. How could this be? Will it continue to deteriorate? What can be done to slow that down? Few of us listen, or even read, with the ambition to understand what the presenter is seeking to divulge to us for the sole purpose of enhancing our world or diverting us from trouble. We are too busy, we really are just too selfish to listen and digest even the words that are given to us with the intention of good. As I have done many times with many other books, you will likely have to read this book more than once to capture even a fraction of what is in it for you. I don't say that to boast about what I've put in it, but as a matter of fact that I have learned through reading books and the Bible myself. The Bible has more to say about our words than almost any other topic in both the old and new testaments. The most respectful thing you can do for anyone, is to genuinely listen to them. Yet, myself included, this is sometimes our most difficult challenge in our busy modern world.

12 The Mission

Does any of this advance the cause of Christ? How does it help people? What am I hoping to communicate? Pick up your bible and read John chapter eight. Jesus spent a considerable amount of time with the Pharisees - the church leaders of his day - trying to convince them of who He was and of His mission. With the Pharisees, He was largely *unsuccessful* - so will I be with many of you. In verse six they sought to deceive him and trap him, but in verse nine they scattered when he forced them to face the truth. They told him that he was lying about who He was in verse thirteen. When He said He was going away in verse twenty-two they thought he might be suicidal. A bit later they seemed to take offense at Jesus suggesting that they were slaves in verse thirty-three. By verse forty-eight they came to the conclusion that He must be demon possessed and therefore by verse fifty-nine we see them picking up stones to throw at Him, but He fled. All of this from just one chapter of one book about how Jesus was perceived among the religious leaders of the day. Even His own family said he was crazy and out of his mind in Mark 3:21. He was indeed radical. His thinking was radical and his life was set apart. I feel compelled to do my best to convince you too, in the same way, of the truth. This book is highly controversial, even provocative, yet I believe it to be God's will for me to share it. It's not controversial based on anything God has said, the source of controversy is based on the traditions of men, the commandments of men, and the ideas of what has become normal among men. Not for my benefit, not for my desire, not for my glory, but for

His good purpose. For God's glory. I only have to know in my heart what God has led me to do and to say. I will ultimately only answer to Him, as will you. We all need to be able to say what Paul said many times to the Jewish leaders of his day, "I have lived my life before God in all good conscience up to this day". (Acts 23:1; 24:16; Romans 9:1; 2 Tim 1:3)

The most important thing that I believe this book can do for you is open your mind to some of the hidden deceptions of the world, but *only* if you're willing. We Christians are probably the world's worst at gathering knowledge and wisdom from great Christian leaders and God's Word and then sitting on it. Proverbs 1:29 says "they hated knowledge and did not choose the fear of the LORD". In other words, they didn't like what they were hearing from God and just chose not to live by it – they didn't fear God in it. If we are not willing to apply any of this great knowledge and understanding to our lives, then it's useless. Perhaps these words can help you to slow down long enough to give thought and discernment to your actions and life with regard to God's Word and His genuine plan for you. By now you know that I'm not talking about the obvious deceptions, but the ones that are disguised and made to seem like good, logical, or even Godly, choices. I don't have it all figured out, but I am urging you to learn to be careful about what you take at face value. Just because it's always been done that way or just because everybody (even Christians) is doing it, doesn't mean it's right or beneficial or even biblical. Paul says in Romans 16:17 - I appeal to you, brothers, to watch out for those who cause divisions and create obstacles contrary to the doctrine that you have been taught; avoid them. To be honest, when I started writing this book many months ago, I had a few selfish ambitions and my personal goals were probably self-serving in many ways. However, through prayer, bible study, and a lot of reading and research, I have read and re-read the text of this book many, many times, and as much as it is possible, God and I have cleaned "me" out of it. Even as I begin to put what I believe are the finishing touches on the pages, I ask God daily to only do with this book what He would have done to bring glory to Him and help as many people as possible. At the same time, some of this content will most certainly strike a nerve with a lot of folks, *especially the women*. But am I now seeking the approval of man, or of God? Or am I trying to please man? If I were still trying to please man, I would not be a servant of Christ. – Galatians 1:10. How many times was Jesus literally chased out of the temple for the things he said? (John 8:59; John 10:39) At this point in writing and reviewing the book, and at this point in my life as a husband, a father, a church member, and a Christ follower, I am simply the messenger. I have no agenda of my own that has not passed through His hands with much prayer and deliberation and counsel. I know and understand that the success or failure of this little project, in terms of its effectiveness, rests totally in the hands of Him anyway – why should I endeavor to do anything *but* His will with it? In a message entitled "Is truth dead", Ravi Zacharias made the statement with regard to our current American culture – "we have picked our own pockets". Toward the end of the message Ravi also says that this is a dangerous time to be alive because there are no definitions. As I began to ponder this in light of the content of this book, I heard the following statements in my mind and heart: In the name of man's definition of beauty, we kill ourselves. In the name of man's definition of modesty, we rape ourselves. In the name of man's definition of happiness, we have made contentment complicated.

Cultures and social norms were never really a concern to God, His law, or Jesus' teachings. However, we certainly saw a lot of culture come into play with regard to the Bible and people and their sin against God. I think you would agree that cultural norms and traditions do not grant us any special permission with God when it comes to obedience. While I can certainly appreciate the diversity of culture and the way it can enhance our lives, I think we have to be careful not to let it rule our lives. Here in the United States, where we have a melting pot of culture and diversity, we sometimes allow those cultural norms to be the rule rather than just an enrichment for people. When we see someone dressing differently or wearing a strange hairstyle or a woman not shaving her armpits, we tend to just point them out and make fun of them. Now sometimes that's because they are exercising practices of their culture that makes them stand out *on purpose*, but more often than not we do this because they're not practicing *our* culture, or the "normal" culture. Please don't hear me saying that I will always get it right, because I may still give a stare at someone I see who is dressed or behaving far outside of what I consider "normal". Like so many of the topics in this book, we really have to make an effort to change what we have considered to be "normal" for most of our lives.

One of my favorite things to do is to watch a storm come in from a distance across a field or body of water. My favorite place to do this is on the western end of Dauphin Island, because you can see in all directions. I even like being in the middle of a storm, unless I'm driving. I hate driving in the beating rain – then I don't like the storm.

Jesus was somewhat about perspective as well. He often used perspective to teach his disciples about his love and his power. When he walked up to them on the water in the middle of a storm, he was challenging their perspective. When he told Peter to step out of the boat, He was wanting to change his perspective. They were all focused on the storm, but when Peter stepped out of the boat, at least for a minute, his perspective was changed. His focus was on Jesus and he trusted that Jesus would protect him from the storm and from sinking into the water and drowning. I imagine that just for a minute, Peter was actually elated to be in the midst of a storm, walking on water toward the Savior. Then just a second later, was frightened to death as he took his eyes off Jesus and again focused on the intensity of the storm.

I think this is where we are as a people in the western world, and especially as a Christian people living in the western world. Our perspective has been shifting for some time now and instead of focusing on Jesus, His Word and our relationship with Him, we have instead shifted our focus to the world and combating the problems that it has created for Christians. We have allowed the world to shift our perspective of sex, of Love, of the human body, of commitment, of prayer, of trust, and even of simple logic and reasoning. We are somehow now looking at the things that God created and called good from a sinful perspective, whereby we now associate many of the perversions of the world with the good of creation. Just because sex has been abused, doesn't make it any less good between a husband and wife. Just because wine has been abused, doesn't make it any less good for moderate consumption into our bodies. Just because greedy people have loved money more than Jesus, doesn't mean that wealth is bad for the believer. Just because the world (and to some degree the church as David Hatton had said) has pornified the human body, doesn't mean that the human body is lewd. This can really be extended to any one of the topics I've covered. We must still be able and willing to call sin out, but we must be very careful that we do not hinder the pursuit of the abundant life for the Christian in the process.

So, this of course begs the question, why do we tend to just go with the flow, with the status quo, with the cultural norm or convention - through the wide gate? And could our following of this wide path in our Christian walk be the cause of some of our spiritual and physical dilemmas? (Matthew 7:13-14) I've touched on those answers in just about every chapter of this book, but what that looks like for you – specifically for your life and practices – could likely be very different from anything I've said, from any topic I've covered. If I had to rank the reasons from top to bottom, I'd say that fear is certainly the number one restriction in one way or another. Fear of the unknown, fear of what people will think or say, fear of being wrong or of failure, fear of challenging the establishment or fear of standing out. Followed closely behind, and in some ways woven into the fear, is embarrassment, shame and uneasiness. If we look at the stories in the Bible in both the old and new testaments, God *never* greatly used anybody who was comfortable. While the disciples may have gotten to a place of comfort as they walked with Jesus and learned from His example, they were all thrust into the unknown as He fulfilled His mission and died, rose and ascended into Heaven, never to physically walk with them again on the earth. Without exception, anyone who was ever mightily used by God was first pulled out of their comfort into the fear of the unknown and the uncommon. I say all of that to say this, while it may not help your fear and discomfort with regard to whatever *radical* adjustments you make in your life as compared to the "normal", you can have some assurance that God can bring you through it, and there will be peace on the other side.

If you look at God's Word, at the stories of war, triumph, desperation, tragedy, surrender and failure, I think you'll agree that living for God and walking with Him is a daily journey. If He is to be a major part of our everyday life, then we must step out in faith and look to Him daily for direction and wisdom. I don't think we can live a life of faith without risk and trials and contemplation. Though to this point in my life I've never met the man, I Love John Eldredge through his books. In the Sacred Romance he says, "It is possible to recover the lost life of our heart and with it the intimacy, beauty, and adventure of life with God. To do so we must leave what is familiar and comfortable - perhaps even parts of the religion in which we have come to trust and take a journey." I cannot agree more with John on this. In fact, the only way, in my opinion, to exercise true faith is by purposefully stepping out of the comfortable and familiar. In order to genuinely trust God, we must have a reason - a risk - to trust Him with. Some purpose that goes beyond our abilities, beyond our practicalities and sophistication, and even beyond our reason and logic and common sense. In several of John Eldredge's books (Wild at Heart, The Sacred Romance, The Journey of Desire), he speaks of God being a wild God or a wild Lover. Just look into a few of the stories in His Word and this becomes perfectly apparent.

The most prevalent, and really the most problematic reason that I see in people who are unwilling to make changes is just a complacency that builds as they get older and more reliant on their way of life to see them through. Thomas Edison once said, "we shall have no better conditions in the future if we are satisfied with all those which we have at present." I would take this a little farther to say that the problems we have today aren't going to just magically vanish if we don't change something about how we deal with them tomorrow.

As I have shared copies of this yet incomplete manuscript for family, friends and people I consider scholars of the Bible to review, it has certainly been *uncomfortable* as I awaited their feedback. Believe me, the writing of this book was the easy part, trusting and hearing from God that what I had put in it was from Him... that was the most trying. As I sat under the great teaching of my pastor and also listened to countless messages from people like David Jeremiah, Robert Jeffress, James Dobson, Chris Hodges, Dr. J. Vernon McGee and many others, I was constantly reading through this book and asking myself – "How many of these topics and ideas lead either to life or destruction?" Anytime you challenge someone's beliefs and way of life, you chance being the recipient of some harsh criticism or ridicule, *especially* with some of the challenges in this little book. As I said in the beginning though, I look forward to the discussion and the criticism, as then at least I will know that people are thinking, questioning, reasoning and working through their chosen ideals and practices in their daily lives. This is indeed the ultimate purpose for the book, and I believe God's will in having me write it. For every little thing we do, in each day that we are given, is a choice... a choice for health, a choice for pleasure, a choice for life, a choice for Love, a choice to be genuine and ultimately a choice for God. The late Joey Feek[42], in a song addressed to God, sang a line that asked, "Did I live all I could live in the time that you gave me?" We should all ask ourselves that very question every day with respect to our marriage, our kids, and especially our God.

I've mentioned the latter part of John 10:10 several times throughout this book in talking about how we should pursue the abundant life, but I've purposefully neglected to mention the first part of the verse until now - The thief comes only to steal and kill and destroy. Think back through all of the topics I've touched on here in terms of both our spiritual and physical condition as people of God. We have *allowed* the thief to steal so much from our lives and *most of us don't even know it.* In fact, most of us have *assisted* the thief in one way or another as he stole, as he destroyed and killed. Will you *choose* to keep helping the thief? In doing so, what harm are you doing to your brothers and sisters in Christ, not to mention the onlookers in the lost world? There is a

---

[42] https://www.youtube.com/watch?v=Mfb6vbCWqYQ

better way. If you don't already know Christ as your savior by accepting his blood sacrifice as a covering for your sin, then you can do that today. If you are already saved by His grace, then you can begin to adjust your lifestyle, your attitude, and your mission to shut down the thief. You don't have to allow him to take anymore, you can choose to live the abundant life that Jesus promised. It's a choice you can make, and He will flat out help you do it.

I don't believe that God is so much interested in the Christian's strict denunciation of every little hint of possible temptation in their life – especially with regard to legitimate personal convictions, but He has proven over and over in scripture that He is mostly interested in our motivations and attitude with regard to His holiness. All throughout the gospels we see the Pharisees time after time exhibiting sinful attitudes with sinful motivations in an effort to "trap" Jesus and catch Him breaking the law. As already mentioned earlier, Jesus even says to them that their problems are on the inside – their cups appear clean on the outside, but on the inside, they're filthy. When it comes to sexuality, nudity, drinking, eating, sleeping, giving, loving, and many other aspects of our daily living, the timing, the motivation, and purpose for our actions often reveal the "good" or the "bad" of our choices. There are so many behaviors that have been labeled as "sin" by the church and many Christians, even though the Bible never condemns them when carried out with the right motivation and within the confines of His Word. How many of your personal convictions were created as a result of an illegitimate culture or deception within the church? If this is indeed the case, should you hold tight to those personal convictions? Sex is certainly a prime example of this. For this reason, your conscience and your convictions can and do change over time and experience. The gray areas of the Christian life, the things that are not specifically prohibited by God must be dealt with carefully and thoughtfully. Paul carefully addresses this in Romans 14 where he talks about food and drink for the culture of the day. We must not allow culture or convention to dictate or shape our conscience, but instead leave room in your life for your convictions to change or vision to see the wrong in them. The sexual crisis of our day is not the agenda of the LGB or LGBT or LGBTQ or LGBTI or the use of pornography or the increase in sex trafficking or child abuse or any other issue you want to point to with regard to sex. These are simply the symptoms of the failure of God's people to embrace and celebrate and praise Him for the gift of our sexuality as designed for marriage. Christian woman, follower of Jesus Christ, husband, preacher, deacon ...wake up! It's time you begin to follow the commands of Christ and as Jesus, Paul, and Peter had to do in their day - rid the church of those who are deceiving you. If what you are taught or told does not line up with the Word of God then it is NOT of God! What is your source of wisdom and knowledge? Man or God? Be careful.

I recently had to have a root canal on a tooth that was causing me constant pain. I am a bit of a wimp when it comes to the dentist and teeth and drilling and pain. I was given a choice of spending a little more money for the use of nitrous to dull the displeasure of the procedure. It was a wise choice for me, but I learned a lot through the process of taking in the nitrous. When you're on the nitrous, you're there but you're not there.

You have some idea of what's going on, but you're certainly not completely coherent. Thus, the benefit of the nitrous for such a procedure. This is kind of what the world can do to a Christian if we let it. It can control us and dim our senses. It will blur the light of God's truth and even cause our hearing to fail amidst the noise around us. If you've ever been taken completely under anesthesia, you understand that you are completely at the mercy of the doctors and nurses once you are out. This is where Satan wants us to be as Christians, knocked out and unconscious to the truth of God's word and will for our lives. Completely under the worlds control where God will be surreal and distant. At a place where we can still know of God and even see Him at times, but yet not live genuinely for Him at all. When we live here, it seems that the lies of the world are so much more comfortable than the truth of God.

Imagine a boy or girl who grew up in a strict and somewhat legalistic Christian home where they were taught that looking upon nudity was strictly sinful. Their conscience, and very likely their Christian personal conviction towards nudity, would then alert them to the slightest temptation or exposure to the nudity of another person as sinful. Now let's suppose that this same boy or girl feels called into the health profession as a doctor or nurse. At some point in this chosen career path, it is very likely that they will have to deal with the naked human body up close and intimately. Without a change in their personal convictions about nudity, how would they possibly do this? My point is this – we have all been raised in a culture and society whereby we have allowed the formation of some personal convictions or conscience about things that clearly do not violate God's

Word. While some of these convictions may have clear links with our past or our experiences that may indeed prevent us from ever transforming our conscience, we must be sure that they aren't just a product of our culture or a product of convention. If they are simply a product of culture or convention, then we must know that we have the liberty in Christ to change! Especially if the resulting changes could have a positive effect on the watching world and lead us down the path of a more abundant life! I believe that the things the Bible does not say are just as important as the wisdom and truth that is written into the words. Perhaps there are many areas of behavior and living that God chose not to strictly and specifically address in his Word because He wasn't so interested in necessarily restricting our behavior, as He is in checking our motivation behind the behavior, examining our heart. (Romans 2) Proverbs 21:2 says every way of a man is right in his own eyes, but the Lord weighs the heart. In like manner, the Word says that we can *appear* to be alive, to be walking with God, to be living for God, and yet be dead (Revelations 3:1). How many of us are doing that, especially within the church, as was the reference in Revelations? How many of us appear to be alive, but we're really dying inside? How many of us just *choose* to be dead? I've been there. *Just going with the flow.* One of my favorite sayings is this - "Any old dead fish can float downstream with the flow, but it takes a live fish to swim against it". Are you judging people or ideas or lifestyle choices without really understanding them, or without sound Biblical reason to do so? The Bible says that a fool takes no pleasure in understanding, but only in expressing *his* opinion, and that if one gives an answer before he hears, it is his folly and shame (Proverbs 18:2, 13). So why do you do what you do? Why do you avoid the things you avoid? What "convictions" do you live by? What is your motivation to do so? Is it Godly? Is it genuine?

Job 28

www.ingramcontent.com/pod-product-compliance
Lightning Source LLC
LaVergne TN
LVHW041155080426
835511LV00006B/602